SOUTHERN NIBLETTS

SOUTHERN NIBLETTS

AN ANTHOLOGY OF SHORT STORIES WRITTEN BY AND ABOUT TWO FAMILIES GROWING UP SOUTHERN

Stories selected and edited by Clifton O. Bingham, Jeanne Weeks Fell and primary author James Edward Fell
Contributing authors; Deanne Weeks Bingham, Jeanne Weeks Fell, Donna Lovelady Pierce, Mattie Grace Pierce, Nancy Fell Murphy, Daniel Joseph Fell, Angela Maria Brumfield
And Santa

This book celebrates the grace and simple elegance of Southern family living.

ISBN 978-1-257-02513-8

Dedication

Everyone has a story to tell, but no one tells a story like a true Southerner.

This book is dedicated to Southerners everywhere who live life and carry on conversations in exclamation marks!

Southern conversations are lively narratives that impart wisdom often without the awareness of the other person, much like subliminal messages.

This book is filled with these stories and dedicated to those story tellers … wherever they may be.

INDEX

INTRODUCTION

So, what are "Southern Nibletts?" For the past year and a half I thought I had made up the word "Nibletts." I was looking for a Southern sounding word to describe the true family stories that I had planned to include in this anthology. That is, I thought it was my word until my wife Googled it. To my surprise and our disappointment, we found someone else had already invented my word, but happy to learn the word was even more Southern than we thought. My intent was to come up with a word that would represent stories of all sizes and subjects, mostly of Southern origin and ones that would be fun for the whole family to read.

As it turns out, the word "Nibletts" may have been the name, or even the nickname, of a Confederate soldier from Texas. There is a small park in Calcasieu Parish about five miles off I-10 near Vinton, Louisiana called Niblett's Bluff. During the Civil War, it was a place where Confederate volunteer soldiers from Texas gathered to travel down the Sabine River on their way to help defend New Orleans. Today, Niblett's Bluff is a park run by the people of Vinton, Louisiana with the motto, "Fun for the Whole Family." I could not have found a more perfect word to describe these stories that were planned for this book. I admit, at first, I had wanted to take a little poetic liberty and call it "Southern Fried Nibletts," but that sounded a too much like a cook book. My wife and I finally choose, "Southern Nibletts" as the perfect description for this collection of true stories written by and about the lives and adventures of our two families, growing up Southern.

I do have a small confession to make. I am only half Southern. I was born in Kansas and raised in Missouri, but my Southern half comes from my wife, Jeanne, who was born and raised deep in the heart of Louisiana along with her twin sister, Deanne. Both she and her sister, who I affectionately call my other wife, have contributed Nibletts to this book. Their stories present beautiful reflections of both their Southerness and their sisterhood.

It is an entertaining experience being married to twins. These girls are identical in every way. They look alike, sound alike, and think alike. Many a time I have picked up a phone and carried on a ten minute conversation with a lady I thought to be my wife, only to discover it was my "other wife". Since it is a well known fact that identical twins have identical DNA, we husbands sometimes jokingly refer to them as "spare parts."

We have also included stories from two up and coming young journalists, my son, Danny, and my daughter, Nancy, which could be considered pure nepotism if it were not for the quality of their writings. My daughter Nancy, is a cancer survivor and while undergoing treatment she started her own writing career with her little e-mail updates called, "Lymph Notes." She buried her pain in humor and her prognosis in undisputable optimism. She always has a way of turning a, "how are you" question into, "You sure look great. How are you doing?" She ends everything she writes with a quotation from Louisa May Alcott's book, "Little Women" that usually appears on the bottom of every page, and will tell you much more about her life than I ever could.

"I'm not afraid of storms, for I am learning to sail my ship."

Nancy teaches hearing impaired children at a school district in central Florida and is totally devoted to her students and her family. Her new Blog, "Because of Daises" is a read well worth your time.

If you have ever been on an airplane with a crying child, especially one that is not yours, you will enjoy Nancy's story, "Cries in the Skies" or a story taken from her Blog, "The Butterfly Effect." They are followed by a story I wrote about her when she was only four, "Ride'm Cow Girl."

My son Danny is the only formally educated writer in the family. He has a journalism degree from the University of Georgia. Danny works for a cable news company in Atlanta, but in his spare time, he is the world's greatest St. Louis Cardinal Baseball fan. The Cardinals won their league and the right to face the Boston Red Sox in the World Series of 2004. Although Danny lived in Atlanta, and our family had left St. Louis when he was only five years old, he made the eight hour car trip without so much as a ticket to a single game, just to be there in St. Louis to support his beloved Cardinals. Unfortunately, Boston swept the Cardinals in four straight games, later to be known as, "The Boston Massacre." Two years later, the

Cardinals won their league again and would face the Detroit Tigers in the World Series. I don't know what made him go this time, but I do remember reading the sports pages where all the writers predicted a Detroit Tiger romp. Although the World Series is a best of a seven game event, several of the sports writers picked Detroit in five, while others were so bold as to pick them in four straight games. Then one arrogant Boston writer, sarcastically picked Detroit in three. I don't know if that was what got him going this time, but he packed his car and headed north.

His contribution to the book comes as a colorful game description in the way of a thank you letter to his brothers. When they heard he was in St. Louis again, they went on the Internet and bought him a ticket to game number four.

Danny's story offers a unique inside look at a true sports fan, and will make you smile or perhaps even cry as you share his once in a lifetime thrill.

If you have ever wondered how men differ from women when it comes to vacations, you will enjoy my description of our recent vacation trip to San Francisco followed by my wife's story about the same trip titled, "What Really Happened." The difference measured in computer terms, was 12,146 KB for her and 26 KB for me. There is enough similarity to know we were both on the same trip, but enough difference to realize, one was written by a man and the other a woman. You be the judge, but as for me: Viva la différence.

Each Christmas, I have tried to document family memories, put them into little booklets, and give them as gifts to each of my five children and my grandchildren. My first venture was to dig out all the old stories about the funny little things that happened to them as they grew up. The following year, I did the same thing, only this time it was about the next generation of little ones, my grandchildren. Last year, I took on a much bigger project of writing a family history, but this time I was the one who got surprised. While doing my research, I discovered the history of those rowdy Irish immigrants on my wife's side and the struggles of my parents during the great depression. Their lives were filled with as much humor as there was tragedy. A fictional writer could never have found material this good. It was a lot of work, but a pleasure to tell their stories, warts and all. I have included a few excerpts from this family history to demonstrate how their lives were filled with the same passions, struggles, and humor as ours, only in another time, and a world away.

If I had a mission in creating this book, it would have been to reveal the grace and the simple elegance of Southern family life. This book of true stories was created for easy and relaxed reading to be enjoyed by the whole family. If you need a little humor in your life read, "Did You Ever See a Dog Smile?" or "Don't Eat The Crabs." But if you prefer a tear or two, read, "Just Me and the Dog" or "The Blood Bank Story." On the serious side, you may want to read, "Sins of Omission" or "My Mother Was A Woman Possessed." To understand what it is like growing up Southern, read Deanne Weeks Bingham's, "Teacakes" or "The Magic Box'. But, don't miss, "Southern Innocence" it is the very first story in our book … for a reason.

I have ended the book with a short letter to all my children that was included in my original family history titled, "This I Believe." This short confession, in just a few words, attempts to pass on all that I have learned about life. The conclusions are based on the experiences and the knowledge gained through my seventy plus years, then offered as a guide to live by. For me, it is a fitting end to this book of true stories, and a timely reminder to all of us, why the family photos are the first thing we save, when there is a threat of danger.

Of all the stories we gathered together for this anthology, there was never a doubt about the one that represented our theme as well as "Southern Innocence" and would be the first to be read.

SOUTHERN INNOCENCE

by James E. Fell

I looked up and to my surprise saw this young girl with long canary yellow hair and beautiful dark eyes staring down at me. Although she wasn't smiling, she didn't appear to be unhappy, just a simple, impatient look that said, "I am ready, let's go, I've been waiting for you." I wanted to turn away with embarrassment as I was sure she had the wrong man, but instead I looked past her dark eyes to her flowered broad brimmed bonnet and her youthful figure. She was as fine an example of true Southerness as one could ever hope to find.

It wasn't until the soft tone of my wife's voice came from across the room asking, "Do you like it?" that I allowed my senses to return to the French Quarter and the little New Orleans art gallery. "It's a Rodrique," she said. "Where is the blue dog," I said? There was a moment of silence as we both carefully searched the canvas background of trees and clouds for a blue dog.

It was a limited silk screen print, Number 66 of 500, thirty by twenty five inches, without frame, and her name was Jolie Blonde. I didn't ask how much it would cost or anything about the high quality 100 pound rag canvas. I just knew for sure, I would be taking her home.

I know very little about art, and as far as I can remember this was the first time I had ever been in an art store with enough money to buy something. Since that fateful day we brought Jolie home, we have gone to Rodrique exhibits and found that Jolie Blonde is not the only painting that has no blue dog. A book we purchased provided some history on the Jolie Blonde painting that surprised me, but in a way authenticated the true southerness I see in my Jolie.

It was one of the early pieces Rodrique had created when after having a hard time finding a market for his paintings, an art teacher suggested he paint the things he was most familiar with. It was on this advice, with no model to guide his brushes, and working all one night, he painted the legendary Jolie Blonde as a young Cajun girl. He painted her under a dark moss laden oak tree near a river. With this painting George Rodrique brought to life the story and song of a pretty Cajun girl that H. Palmer Hall describes as “a fantasy teased out of the muddy waters of the Atchafalaya River.” This fantasy came wrapped in traditional Cajun music that had been written some fifty years earlier in a Texas prison. Some call it the Cajun Waltz or Cajun Anthem, but the real name in French is “Ma Blonde Est Parti” a song about Jolie Blonde, a pretty young girl who had left her Cajun lover for another man.

Needing money to continue his work, but not wanting to sell Jolie, he sold a license to use the painting as a photograph along with the name, “Jolie Blonde” to a group of entrepreneurs. They were opening a new brewery and wanted her picture and name for the label of their new beer. They actually called it Jolie Blonde Beer, and made it right there in South Louisiana. The brewery lasted only two years, which placed my Jolie back upon the pedestal where she belonged. I later found a poster for Jolie Blonde Beer on eBay and purchased it, not so much to have it to display, but to take it out of circulation and maintain the dignity of my Jolie Blonde. Today a new Jolie Blonde Beer is being brewed by a New Jersey Brewery, and I am not sure I will have enough money to buy up all their posters, but I may try.

I am told these prints increase in value over the years as the artist gains fame making their early paintings special collector items. They also gain value as many of the limited prints are lost or damaged over the years. Rodrique, having first gained fame with his “blue dogs,” has since established himself as a worldwide artist, and is much in demand. Right after 9/11, he created a painting he called “God Bless America” and almost immediately sold 1000 limited edition prints, raising over $500,000.00 for the victim’s families. Since that time, he has raised even more money to help the victims of Hurricane Katrina.

I don’t know how many of his original paintings or the limited prints of Jolie Blonde, may have been lost or destroyed since Hurricane Katrina, or what the true value is today, but she is home now, here in the south, with us, where she belongs. I can assure you … no amount of money will ever take our Jolie away.

One Saturday morning about three years ago I got up thinking about my mom, sat down at the breakfast table and watched my pen write the words, "My Mother Was A Woman Possessed." I feel it appropriate to add, I kept on writing until the story that follows was finished and allows me to give you a special insight into the life of a very special woman, my mother.

MY MOTHER WAS A WOMAN POSSESSED

by James E. Fell

In a nice way, my mother was a woman possessed. In her case she was possessed with many secret talents. Because of her shyness and fear of almost anything that moved, including thunder storms, large crowds and cars that went over 30 miles per hour, her talents remained well hidden. Very few people knew of theses hidden abilities or fears, with the exception of her immediate family and one very close friend.

Her mother, my grandmother Routh (pronounced Ruth), was a widow who raised her five children by teaching piano to anyone who would pay, which of course, excluded her own children. My mother would sit and listen to other children struggle through their first two-handed tunes, making sounds that would hurt your ears and seldom would allow you to identify the melody. My mother would wait until the lesson was over and the student had left, then sit down and play the tune the way it was written, plus a few frills of her own. At that time, playing by ear was looked upon as something akin to plagiarism or bootlegging and my mother was rewarded with a smack across the fingers with a wooden ruler.

Her other talents included song writing, poetry, and lyrics to songs that had none, as well as replacing lyrics to songs with bad lyrics. I only know most of this because I ran across these well hidden treasures, stuffed away under some music books and magazines, in the home of my mother's best friend, Frieda. Most of the good things have been lost, but then none of this would have ever come to light had I not stopped by to visit my Mom's best friend, who still lived in that small Oklahoma town where I grew up. I was in the Army at the time, completing my final training, just a few miles away from my mom's friend. We had the weekend off and a party was out of the question in a dry state like Oklahoma, so we went sightseeing. I was showing my friends the little town in Oklahoma where I had spent the better part of my youth.

During World War II my Mom worked in the government office that issued food and gas rationing stamps. She and her soon-to-be best friend, Frieda, met when one of them dialed a wrong number and started a conversation, discovering they both worked on different floors in the same building. They also discovered they were both piano players, but otherwise, total opposites. Frieda was outgoing, loved crowds, and knew no fear. Having played the piano or organ for every wedding party or funeral in that little town, she knew absolutely all the dirt on most everyone that was worth knowing and a few that weren't.

I remember during the war years our little town in the heart of Oklahoma was in no way isolated from the conflict. We had a flight school that trained new pilots, not only for us, but men from England's Royal Air Force and other allied countries. They built an Army hospital for the returning wounded, and we even had a prisoner of war camp full of German and Italian prisoners from the battles in Africa. As a young man growing up and not knowing the ugly side of war, it all seemed like a very exciting time for both me and for my family. I had a paper route and I can still remember delivering 144 copies of the Daily Express each afternoon on my bicycle and on week ends getting up at 4 AM to deliver the big Sunday issue. I still remember the things a young man sees at four in the morning, riding through the streets and alleys, in a small town full of soldiers who are trying to live each Saturday night like it might be their last. I remember the German prisoners who would stand by the tall barbed wire fence next to our baseball field and speak to us in broken English about their sons or daughters at home in Germany. They would cheer for us and call us by name as we played ball.

But most of all, I remember my Mom and Frieda playing piano at the Army hospital to entertain the troops. The hospital was the last stop on my paper route and I would ride fast to deliver all my papers so I could spend a little time listening to them play. Sometimes big bands and entertainers like Bob Hope and other movie stars would come to entertain, but that was mostly at night and I wasn't there. Years later, when I visited Mom's friend, she told me how my Mom could write music or would hear a new song for the first time, hummed or whistled by one of the wounded soldiers. After hearing only a few bars, she would start playing and even finish the song. When asked how she did that, in her shy way she would simply say, "I knew how the rest of the song went because, that's the way it had to be." It sounds a little like Gracie Allen, but that was my mom.

It reminded me of the time she was trying to teach me how to drive a shift car by telling me to "just push down on that pedal next to the one that stops the car and count to four while you let it up." I asked her what the name of that pedal was, just for fun, and she said, "It really doesn't make any difference, the important thing is how fast you count to four." Now, after many years of driving shift cars, I am beginning to think she was right.

My newspaper route was for the same newspaper where my Mom had worked twelve years earlier as a feature writer. I never saw any of the things she wrote, but those who did said she was more than just good, she had a style that was fresh and new. When given a very dull subject to feature, she somehow ended up making it both interesting and humorous, which is most likely why they took her off her first assignment of writing obituaries. She quit the newspaper to get married, but Frieda said she had a real future in writing. While she worked at the newspaper, she also sang with her sister on the small town radio station and that is where she met my dad. He was working with a construction crew on a new bank building, heard her on the radio, and went to the studio to meet her. You might call it "love at first sound," but no matter what you call it, my sister and I were the result, along with the worst depression that the modern world had ever seen. Fifteen years later, as if waiting for the tough times of the depression and the war to be over with, my brother, Jay, was born.

It wasn't long after Jay was born that I was off to college and then to the Army. My basic officer training was near the little Oklahoma town where I grew up, where my mother played the piano, and where we all survived World War II.

A free weekend during my training gave me an opportunity to renew an old acquaintance with my Mom's best friend, and in turn learn more about my Mom than I had known as a child growing up. I had five fellow officers who had come along on the weekend to see the town and the World War II history I had told them about. We had only planned to stop and say hello to Frieda, but our hello turned into a long weekend when she sent us to the store for some ribs to bar-b-que, while she called the local college and talked to a group of young girls she had worked with to come over, providing all the makings for a party. When we got back with the food one of the guys asked why Oklahoma was a dry state and what did that mean? Frieda's answer was, "it just means the booze costs less because there is no state tax and it is delivered to your door, instead of having to go to a liquor store and pick it up." The young lieutenant thought she was putting him on and just laughed. Frieda picked up the phone dialed a number, handed him the phone, then said, "Place your order." He did, and ten minutes later a taxi cab drove up, the door bell rang, and the party was underway.

After the girls left and my friends crashed on the couch, floors, and empty beds, Frieda and I dug through all her old papers, music books, and scrapbooks, reading her writings and listening to the stories of Frieda and Mom's war adventures. Frieda told me about the songs Mom had written and played them for the professional musicians who came to the hospital with the entertainers. They seldom traveled with a piano or a piano player, so they would hire a local one or get volunteers like Mom to sit in. Frieda said Mom never thought her songs were good enough to get published, however, several of her songs did get published, but not in her name. Frieda said that happens all the time when you play your songs for other musicians and there is not much you can do about it. She said Mom recognized the melody, but instead of being mad, she was just happy someone finished it and got it played.

My mom is gone now, but she left a husband and, as she often said, three ***almost*** perfect children. As for me, I will always think of her each time I hear one of those old World War II songs, and each time I drive a shift car, remembering to count to four as I let up on that pedal with no name.

Sooner or later every college student gives a serious thought to God and what part, if any, He may play in the rest of their lives. For me, that thought came quite by accident.

SINS OF OMISSION

by James E. Fell

We had just discovered that our new friend and frequent player in our never ending student union card game was a Catholic priest. His unintentional disguise was effective even though he was a few years older than the rest of the students who hung out at the student union. In the late forties, returning veterans were all a few years older, so when we needed a fourth for bridge, we never gave it a thought as we invited them to join in. As for the clothes, he explained that he was taking a few courses at the university and normally did not wear his priestly garb to class just to avoid drawing attention to himself. As he put it, clothes don't make him a priest, but his words and actions do. Only this day he had no choice. He had a funeral mass and with no time to change, he wore his black suit with the Roman collar. We were all so convinced he was a student just like us that one of our card game game regulars asked, in all sincerity, if he was going to a masquerade party.

Once the shock and laughter subsided, we each began to recall all the four letter words we had used in the past two weeks along with any sins we may have been bragging about while the cards were being dealt. None of us were Catholic, however we each had our favorite Catholic story to tell, especially since we had this captive audience. Father Tom patiently listened and in most cases laughed with us. Jokes and stories were followed by a few questions, mostly about his background along with the inevitable question; "Why did you become a priest?" His answer was quick but sincere; "Because I wanted to serve God." Then, out of the blue, but most likely just to show off his Latin skills, one of the players asked the priest what the "Confiteor" was. Father Tom looked a little surprised, but then explained how each mass is started with a prayer called the Confiteor, which is Latin and means, "my confession." He said "Everyone in the church including the priest recites the prayer aloud. It is a very short prayer but has always been one of my most treasured parts of the mass." After a short pause, he looked up and softly recited the prayer.

"I confess to Almighty God and to you my brothers and sisters, that I have sinned through my fault, in what I have done and what I have failed to do. I ask blessed Mary, ever virgin, all the angles and saints, and you my brothers and sisters, to pray for me to the Lord our God."

A moment of silence followed, not only by our regular players, but others near by who had been listening. Thinking things had gotten a bit too serious, I interrupted with a humorous quip. "Wouldn't you know, if there was more than one way to commit a sin the Catholics would be the first ones to find it?" I don't recall much more about that day, but those words from his prayer, "what I have failed to do," have stayed with me all these years.

Father Tom and I became good friends and we had many a discussion about religion and as I called it, "the second kind of sin," or as he called it, "the sins of omission." He admitted to me that, for a priest, the religious life presents almost daily occasions for the sins of omission. "For us they are a constant reminder not to miss those special opportunities to recognize the living God that is present in all our lives and in each person we meet." As he explained, "It is easy to get caught up in the routine of your office and fail to recognize a duty to act." I asked him how anyone could ever recognize those occasions and what he said, although confusing at the time, years later became my constant moral companion. He told me that "God lives in all of us and if we just concentrate on seeing the good in every living creature we meet, no matter how good or bad they may appear, we will never need to worry about the sins of omission."

When the time came for my graduation I received my commission in the Army and my orders the same day telling me I would not be able to be there for the graduation ceremony and that they would mail my degree to me. On my way out of town I went by to say goodbye to Father Tom only to find he also had his orders. He was going to Rome to become a Canon lawyer. With the Korean War still going, we were most likely headed to opposite ends of the world, but we parted with hope that someday we would meet again, but we never did.

In the eight years that followed, I got my degree in the mail as promised, served my country in the Army, came home, met a wonderful lady and got married. I had a job with a large construction company and had just received a promotion to run my first big project as the boss, the man in charge.

I was younger than most of the workers, but things were going well at my project. I was right on budget and ahead of schedule. Even though I was half the age of many of the workers, my strategy was to make things happen by being easy to talk to, a good listener, a fair minded boss, and most importantly, I presented myself as just one of the boys.

About once a week lunch time on a construction project becomes a special occasion. It is an outdoor picnic that in some ways should remind you of the lunches you had in grade school where all the kids would compare their sandwich with what the other kids had in their lunch pail. Just like the kids, the construction site is also a ritual of comparisons. It is an unveiling of what one wife has prepared to impress your fellow workers only, unlike grade school, this is the major leagues of comparisons. Hoots and hollers follow each presentation along with a number of four letter expletives. At this project the men had claimed the top of the concrete retaining wall that ran along the railroad tracks as their noon day banquet table. They would straddle the wall and lay out their lunch on the top of the wall in front of them. For such noonday events your presence was only noticeable by your absence. This is why I always attended, but never participated.

It was on one of these days that Big Jake was at the top of his act trying to start an argument with one of the carpenters over who had the best meatball sandwich. After the normal bragging about how good a cook his wife was and the carpenter's retort that only an Italian wife like his should be allowed to make meat ball sandwiches. The workers voted with cheers or boos as each sandwich was raised on high. It ended in a draw, as they all do and after the food was gone another contest was started. Turned around facing the far side of the tracks they started with rock throwing across the tracks into an old rusted barrel full of water. Cheers would go up each time a rock would cause a splash as it hit the water with lots of oohs and ahs for the near misses. Since the retaining wall had been backfilled with medium sized white rocks, all within picking distance of their perch on top of the wall, there was little chance that running out of ammunition would stop the show.

Over the loud cheers and boos coming from the rock throwers, I heard the distant sound of singing. It became louder as a tall bearded man in tattered clothes and singing, continued walking towards us on the tracks. Except for me, no one else paid much attention to the singing man or his beautiful baritone voice. As I listened to the hymn he sang and judged his pace, it became obvious his pathway would soon interfere with the rock throwing. When the men finally noticed, they began swearing at him and yelling for him to get off the tracks and stop his singing. The man looked up, said nothing, but stopped singing and hurried past the rusted barrel and down the tracks out of harms way. Once again he continued his journey and his singing. I had never in my life heard such a beautiful voice, but apparently I was the only one so moved. Bored with the barrel game, some of the men once again began to yell at him and playfully at first, began to toss rocks his way, coming close, but few hitting him. Then, with more yelling and more men getting involved, some rocks unintentionally were hitting him obviously causing pain. He pulled the hood of his tattered coat above his head for protection and once again hurried down the tracks until he was out of range, where he stopped and turned to face us. Then in a soft but commanding voice he asked, "Why do you hurt me? I have done nothing to you." After a moment of pure silence, he slowly turned away and moved down the tracks, then after a short time we all heard that beautiful hymn in the distance as he continued his journey.

Not much was said after that. The men quietly returned to their work. The rest of the day was very unusual. The men actually appeared to be going out of their way to be helpful to me and to each other as if trying to make up for something they had done. I, on the other hand, was still bothered knowing that I, as the boss, could have stopped the rock throwing at any time. The fact that no one was really hurt or seriously injured didn't seem to mater for me or the men. I realized I had been so intent on trying to be "Mr. Nice Guy" and let the "boys be boys," that I had failed to see pure goodness when I met it face to face. I immediately thought of father Tom and knew he would have told me that the workers' sin was one of commission; throwing the rocks along with the verbal abuse but my sin was the sin of omission, for not having stopped it when I had the chance. Now, I am reminded of that day each time I hear a beautiful hymn or see a homeless person.

A few years ago when I returned to St.Louis to visit my daughter, I found time to drive by and look for the place where we had built that first building, even though I had heard the building had been torn down to make way for a big new office park. Although the building was gone, I was not surprised to see those same railroad tracks leading to Kansas

City and all points West. Next to the tracks I could still see that big concrete retaining wall where the construction workers ate their lunch. It was all still there, right where we left it ... forty six years ago.

The Teacake poem was written by Deanne Weeks Bingham, as a tribute to her grandmother and grandfather. Her poem tells a story that reflects the beautiful relationship southerners have with their elders and the respect they have for traditions,.. even the ones as small as "Teacakes".

TEACAKES, GRANNY AND THE PREACHER

by Deanne Weeks Bingham

She is just a wee little person, only four foot eleven
A bundle of energy sent to our family from heaven
To spend her life taking care of our clan
With a broom and a bowl and an iron in her hand.

The summers she spent with us were filled with delight
As she sewed and she stitched way into the night
Getting my sister and me ready for school in the fall
And always reminding us we were growing so tall.

Then she would braid our hair
so tight that our eyes wouldn't close.
We couldn't laugh or smile
or even wiggle our nose.

We loved watching her nightly tradition
Getting brushes and combs and pins in position
She'd take her hair down from the coil on her head
And brush it slowly before going to bed.

With long lovely strokes she'd carefully braid
Then proudly show us the design she had made.

She would spend hours and hours starching fluffy white shirts
So Granddad, the Preacher, would look good in church.
He stood in that pulpit with dignity and grace
While the glow of the Father shined bright on his face.

Granny was always at his side in her place
Even if he didn't need her, she was there, just in case.
He'd stand straight and tall and loudly proclaim
"Praising the Lord is important, nothing else is the same."

We'd sit there in church so quiet and so sweet
As we wondered if Granny had teacakes to eat.
We patiently waited for the final "Amen"
And rushed back to Granny's for teacakes again!

Here is another beautifully told story by, Deanne Weeks Bingham, about growing up Southern, as two little twin girls discover the magic in their aunt's mysterious red box.

THE MAGIC BOX

by Deanne Weeks Bingham

Weary from her day's work, she stood and stretched her tired back.
Her fingers were stained purple from the shelling of peas.
Her apron - faded and worn.

She glanced suddenly at the clock by the door, as if some unheard alarm had just sounded.
It was half-past-four o'clock and only moments before her "knight in shining armor" would arrive home from work.
He would be unaware of her hard work that day and she could not greet him in her tired old apron and her hair in pin curls.

She rushed to the small powder room off the hall.
Following her closely were two barefoot little girls with blonde ponytails.
They watched lovingly as she changed from her work clothes to her best cotton dress.
She quickly pulled the pins from her hair and brushed out her curls that fell just below her shoulders and framed her pretty face.
She was finally ready for the magic.

She took a tiny red box from the cupboard behind a mirror on the wall.
The box had a curious inscription that the girls had never before seen.
It read – "Maybelline!"
She removed a small red brush, dampened it and dabbed the brush in the cosmetic within the red box. Then, she artfully brushed her golden eyelashes with the magical potion and separated each tiny lash, then arched perfect eyebrows from the same little brush.

The two little girls stared – intrigued!
When she was satisfied with her reflection in the mirror she placed the brush back in its little red box and returned it to its place inside the cupboard behind the mirror on the wall.

With a final dash of color to her lips and a pinch to her cheeks she glanced into the mirror for one last look.
She had been transformed from an ordinary housewife into an elegant lady.

She heard a sound from far down the road – a sound that only she could have heard.
It was the sound of his old pickup truck.
A smile played with her mouth as she gazed out the window and with a sparkle in her eyes she dashed out to meet him.
The little girls giggled with delight!

It would be years before they would understand her secret. The magic was not in the tiny red box, but in the heart of the woman who loved this man so dearly.
It was her love for him that transformed the ordinary housewife into the beautiful and elegant lady.

Written with love
In commemoration of the 50th Wedding Anniversary
Of Marshall and Louise Nelson

It was more than just strange, it was real. I saw two living breathing saints. I am 100% sure I did, but before you start thinking of me as some kind of religious fanatic who sees visions and spouts prophecy, I want you to know, I am simply your average, or slightly below average, everyday sinner. You don't need to be anyone special to see what I saw, you just need to be in the right place at the right time and know where to look. Let me show you how it works.

A STRANGE THING HAPPENED ON THE WAY TO THE BLOOD BANK

by James E. Fell

One Sunday after mass, some volunteers for our church blood drive cornered my wife, Peggy, and asked if she would help. Peggy, knowing full well that they never take blood from pregnant woman, said, "Sure. WE would love to," and immediately volunteered my blood. Allowing my male ego to take possession of my body for a short minute, I mustered a big masculine smile and said, "Sure, where do I sign up?" What the heck, it wasn't for two weeks and just think of all the things that could happen in two weeks, like catching a cold, going on a business trip, or just plain forgetting. Well it was the forgetting that got me. I really did forget, but my wife didn't, and even worse, waited until the last minute to remind me. What could I do? I went!

As far as I am concerned, when it comes to giving blood, there are only two kinds of people; those who do it with a smile, but are really scared to death, and those who are scared to death, but go to great lengths to lie about how easy it is. I confess I belong to the first group of liars, but then most men do. Well, anyway, here I was standing in a line to donate what I had always considered to be a critical part of my body. I was looking forward to the next few minutes with about as much enthusiasm as one about to receive an IRS tax audit. I made it through the general health interview with no pain. The woman who did the interview was one of the more saintly woman of our parish. She had nine children of her own, some still in diapers, but like my wife, she was always helping the church or someone with a crisis, wherever she was needed. I couldn't help but notice the small bandage on her inner arm that told me she had survived what I was about to go through and it gave me enough courage to go to the next station.

This was the one where they take a drop of blood from your finger and the person behind the needle was an ex-nurse as well as my next door neighbor. She convinced me that when she stuck that pin in my finger, it would hurt her more than it would hurt me. She is such a sweet, compassionate person, I think it really did hurt her more, but that didn't stop me from looking for the hole in the other side on my finger. As I moved further down the line, I couldn't help but notice the sign above the desk: "LAST STOP" and remember thinking to myself, what a poor choice of words.

It was here that I encountered my first non-volunteer, an honest to goodness professional nurse. Professional was truly the word for her. It took but a minute observing her to know I was fortunate to be witnessing a master craftsman at work. Surely you have had the feeling when seeing a person who is so good at what they are doing it becomes a pleasure just to watch them work. I watched as she dispatched the people in front of me. It was like magic the way she would take one look at them, as if her mind was a "Freudian" program in an invisible computer. She immediately knew the ones who were scared and the ones who were lying about being scared. She treated each a little differently, always saying the right thing to put them at ease or expediting them with an almost unconcerned attitude that served to bolster their lying egos. She divided her attention among her patients as though being controlled by a master time clock, always hurried but never missing a stroke; plug in this one, unplug that one, with an air of confidence that made me willing enough when my time came. She handled me with the same efficiency, telling me there was too much muscle in my right arm, so I should "flip it over, big boy, let's try the other one." I no sooner got turned around than she had me plugged in and on my way to becoming a "Donor."

I am one of the lucky ones over forty with very low blood pressure, only this day it worked to my disadvantage since it served only to prolong my agony. It took but a minute for my life to pass before my eyes and I soon found myself with nothing to do but squeeze the wooden bar and look around the room. It seemed ironical that the new donors standing in line were, for the most part, the people in the parish that could least afford the time and many, by age and size, could least afford the blood. Of course there were a few show-offs who came in jogging togs or tennis outfits. They were the more obvious of the group two liars.

It was at this point that I noticed a young boy in his late teens at the interview table. I had seen him many times before at mass. He always sat with his parents in one of the very front pews. I recalled watching him go to communion and noticing the deep concentration and piety in his face that only the pure of heart possess. Friends of mine who had also noticed the same unique characteristics in this young man told me he was the son of one of the members of our parish and although he was in fine physical condition, he had been both deaf and mute from birth. I watched as he went through the various stations. There was not a single emotion hidden from his face. You could see fear, pride, and above all his courage. He fit none of my stereotype blood donors and I admonished myself in my thoughts for having left honesty and love out of my equation. I lost sight of him for awhile and the next time I saw him, he was first in line to donate. This is when the eyes of my most efficient lady met his, and it was like the world just stopped. In a fraction of a second, somewhere in her marvelous mind, she managed to sum up the situation. With a very noticeable change of pace almost to a point of slow motion, she walked over to him, took him by the hand, and as gently as a first time mother holds her child, she helped him onto one of the tables. Although none of us could hear a word she said, she talked looking straight into his eyes while he managed a faint smile almost like he heard and understood her words. Soon he was plugged in and she was about the rest of her duties, but somehow always at his side. Soon he was finished and she came to his table and helped him set up. She had an expression of exceptional pride and so did he. No words were spoken, but after another of those magical moments he put his arms around her and she returned his thankfulness with a strong hug and a very understanding smile. Giving one of her assistants a gesture to take over for a few minutes, she took him by the hand and walked to the rest and recoup station where, as I promised you, I saw two living saints sit, and laugh, and drink orange juice together.

As I was being unplugged by the assistant nurse, I tried once again to picture the two of them as they walked towards the rest station. I could have sworn I had seen tears in each of their eyes, but then I'm not sure. It's like I told the nurse when she taped the red badge of courage to my inner arm, "Giving blood always makes my eyes water."

When we finally broke away from our "way too busy, work a day routines," to take what we planned to be a "Perfect Vacation," my wife insisted I write a story documenting our ten day adventure to San Francisco and Lake Tahoe. When I finished it, I proudly put it on her computer via e-mail and she wasted no time in telling me I got it all wrong. I told her to write her own story and she did. Here they both are; you be the judge.

OUR CALIFORNIA DREAM VACATION FOR TWO

OUR DREAM VACATION

by James E. Fell

Picture this: You are on a big, beautiful jet, sitting in first class, with a beautiful wife and your very own DVD player, getting ready to take off for a care free week in San Francisco topped off by a long weekend at Lake Tahoe. That's how our dream week in California began.

This was not just one of those ***regular*** bankrupt airline jets where the first class passengers get to board first, sip their pre-takeoff cocktails, and inspect the less fortunate as they struggle back to their way-too-small seats. No sir, this was one of those big new jobs where you enter and a smiling head tells you "first class to the left and 'peons' to the right, Talk about nice, those seats were so large that Jeanne and I both stretched out our legs as far as we could and we still couldn't touch the seat in front of us. We had our own little TV screen and entertainment center built right into each seat. This was not just one of those regular bankrupt airlines; it was DELTA, a recently bankrupt airline!

Just as we settled in and began to enjoy our new-found luxury, Jeanne notices that the dark haired, unshaven man who appears to be of Arab descent, seated in the middle section just to my left, "looks suspicious." She said she heard him order a Bloody Mary, then smiles and says "a bad guy wouldn't do that, would he?" Just to keep her going, I said "no, but maybe he won't drink it. He just ordered it to make you think he was a regular guy." With that said, our suspect got up and walked towards the cockpit door, stood there for a moment, and then entered the restroom just to the left of the pilot's door. I went back to my magazine, but Jeanne never took her eyes off that bathroom door until he reappeared, in what seemed like an eternity later.

Jeanne went back to her Kindle. I continued playing with my private TV, stereo and GPS monitor. I discovered this GPS was showing us a graphic display of our trip with a little symbol of an airplane moving across a map of the United States showing Kansas City, Denver, the Rocky Mountains, and The Grand Canyon with all other cities and points of interest noted. It even showed our heading, air speed and altitude. Now, my attention went back to our suspicious looking mystery man. It became obvious to me, he didn't need knives, or guns, or explosives to do us in. All he needed was his cell phone, a first class seat with a GPS and the guts to disobey the flight attendant's first commandment, "Thou shall never ever operate your cell phone during the flight." Maybe that is why he went to the men's room, so she couldn't see him make the call to his accomplice on the ground with the ground-to-air missile and give him our vital signs of heading, airspeed and altitude. Then his friend feeds the GPS information into his ground-to-air missile.

Well, no sense bothering Jeanne with all this technical information.

She would just say, "I told you so."

Today the United States of America is full of closely spaced little white puffy clouds that look like cotton ball stepping stones from 30,000 feet above them. I love to look out the windows of airplanes, but I don't think that's the cool thing to do. The frequent flyer guys, at least the older ones, sit in the aisle seats or pull the little window shade down so they can appear to be asleep or bored. The younger ones do the same thing, but driven by that $5.00 cup of Starbucks coffee, whip out their laptops and start working. They go at it with an intensity that makes you think one of those older dudes who is pretending to be asleep may be their boss.

They have just announced that we are going to enjoy a Batman movie, free if you brought your own earphones, or $2.00 if you didn't.

I don't remember anyone from my bankrupt airline telling me to bring earphones, but what the heck, I brought my own DVD player and my own movie, better than theirs and besides, I have a beautiful wife.

Apparently the "would be terrorist" got a busy signal on the other end of his cell phone call, or he ran out of minutes, because we made it to San Francisco and our dream vacation, where we fully intended to leave our mark. As a matter of fact, the very first thing we did was to walk from our hotel, next door, to the Top of the Mark. We took the elevator to the top floor overlooking the San Francisco skyline. And there at sundown, in our seats by the window overlooking the bay, we had champagne and caviar, with the photos to prove it.

As part of our planned adventure, we rode every cable car route in San Francisco for two days. The cable car operators called us by name. I was "Tourist" and Jeanne was "Pretty Lady". We rode to Pier 19, the Farmer's Market and China Town. We attended mass at a Chinese Catholic church and shopped 'til we dropped. We sat and sampled Chinese tea served by a teenage Chinese girl who was working her way through medical school and in perfect California English, admitted she never drank the stuff, but managed to sell us $20 worth of tea to take home.

We met my brother Jay and his wife Joan who lived in nearby Tracy on our last day. We got the super 1st class tour of the city including our namesake, Fell Avenue, the bank Pattie Hurst robbed, Lombard Street, Haught Ashbury and finished the day with dinner at a unique little restaurant under the Oakland Bay bridge with a panoramic view of Alcatraz in the background.

From San Francisco we flew to Reno, Nevada, rented a cute little red convertible and drove from the desert straight up the mountains to Lake Tahoe. We drove through a real live snow storm on the way up the mountain, stayed at the Hyatt hotel, won a lot of money playing roulette using our kid's birthdays, (thanks kids) then gave it all back the next night rolling the dice.

We don't remember much about the trip back home. We were too tired. We had purchased black and white striped prison uniforms when we toured Alcatraz, with lettering that identified the "Alcatraz Swim Team and their motto, Swim for your life." We had planned to wear them to Jimmy and Carolyn's Halloween party on the night of our return to Destin, but we were so tired, we converted the prison outfits into pajamas and wore them to bed.

Jeanne fell asleep dreaming about the wonderful feather bed pillow she left in our San Francisco hotel while I went to sleep trying to figure out, whatever happened to that guy's cell phone call? We both agreed – our home here in Destin, truly is Paradise!

OUR DREAM VACATION

by Jeanne Fell

(WHAT REALLY HAPPENED)

Whew! By the time I had packed enough clothes and shoes for an entire week in San Francisco and Lake Tahoe, cleaned the house for our return, loaded the car, and re-checked the front door lock again, I was ready for a vacation.

We had opted for the luxury of first class tickets for the three and one half hour flight. On takeoff we circled out over Destin and the shimmering Gulf of Mexico with a gazillion dazzling diamonds twinkling up from the azure water. Looking down from 10,000 feet, it was so beautiful I was reluctant to leave this Paradise.

The weather was perfect for a cross country flight. Jim was thrilled with all the gadgets the airline provided. He had a GPS at his fingertips and his personal entertainment center and was preoccupied with it during most of the flight. I had just settled down to enjoy my current novel when over to the left in the mid-section, I observed two males of Arab descent sitting quietly not even speaking to each other and looking very suspicious. I was somewhat relieved when the one on the aisle ordered a Bloody Mary since I had read somewhere that terrorists don't drink alcohol. I was most concerned that they ignored each other and stared straight ahead. I whispered to Jim that I thought they were suspicious-looking. He just smiled at me in his patronizing way and turned his attention back to his electronic toys.

I tried to concentrate on my book, but couldn't help keeping this guy in my peripheral vision at all times. At one point he abruptly got up from his seat and walked to the men's room just to the left of the pilot's door. He was in there for what seemed like an eternity then returned to his seat and didn't move again for the remainder of the flight.

Our approach to the airport was beautiful, coming in just above San Francisco Bay. It felt as though the plane was just skimming the water. We claimed our luggage and got a cab and we were on our way to explore the City By The Bay! Hello San Francisco! The temperature was a balmy 60°F during the day and the 50's after sunset. Perfect!

Our hotel, poised on the crest of Nob Hill, was lovely with huge lobby murals depicting scenes of pre-earthquake San Francisco.

The domed ceiling was glorious with huge stained-glass inserts in true Victorian colors and design. But the best surprise was in our room. We had two huge, soft, fluffy, down-filled beds looking out onto California Street with a lovely old cathedral in view from one direction and the Mark Hopkins Hotel just across the street in the other direction.

We asked the concierge to recommend restaurants within walking distance ***DOWNHILL*** from our hotel. As soon as we unpacked we headed straight to the legendary Top of the Mark sky bar next door, and shared a noble bottle of champagne and the restaurant's finest Russian caviar, as we enjoyed the panoramic view of the San Francisco skyline from 20 floors up in the sky.

It was difficult leaving those snuggly, cloud-nine beds the next morning, but we could hear the cable cars announcing their routes. Our hotel was at the crossing of three cable car lines. After breakfast, of the most delicious clouds of lemon soufflé pancakes (with raspberry syrup!) this side of heaven served in the hotel restaurant, we were off to a day of exploring.

We purchased a day pass on the cable cars, and soon were on first name basis with our favorite cable car guy, Wayne. As we rode the hills he entertained us with stories of San Francisco, and even glimpses of his own personal life. I loved this story: It seems that his wife asked for a new handbag for her birthday. He tells her okay, he will buy her a new purse for her birthday. When they get to the store, the one she selects is $700! He tells her there's only one woman in the world he would pay that much for a purse for, and that's his mother! "Who else would let you in anytime of the night, make you something to eat and put you to bed, no matter what, no questions asked?" The cable car guys have a subculture all their own. They keep a running dialogue with each other as they pass time and time again on their same boring routes each day.

We began our walking tour at Fisherman's Wharf. This area began as the logical place for fishermen of the post-Gold Rush boomtown of San Francisco to anchor their boats. As we strolled the streets, the aroma of fresh seafood was overwhelming and I salivate over the fresh Dungeness crab and the crab chowder cooking in outdoor pots everywhere along the piers. We visited The Cannery (Del Monte original cannery in 1907) but now houses trendy shops and restaurants, Ghirardelli Square – famous for their chocolate, and explore Pier 39 and many of the flea market stalls nearby.

The next day we head for Alcatraz. Out in the middle of the San Francisco Bay, the island of Alcatraz is a world unto itself. Isolation, one of the constants of island life for any inhabitant is the recurrent theme in the history of Alcatraz. Visitors to the island can explore the remnants of the prison...

Alcatraz was home to Al Capone for over four years. Influence and privilege were lost at Alcatraz where Capone was assigned menial jobs and treated like everyone else. In failing health due to syphilis, he was transferred to another prison in 1939.

Thirty-six prisoners were involved in escape attempts: 7 shot and killed, 2 drowned, 5 unaccounted for, the rest recaptured. Two prisoners made it off the island but were returned. In June 1962, Morris and the Anglin brothers were successful in escaping both the institution and attempted the swim, but survival is very questionable.

We purchased black and white striped prison uniforms with "Alcatraz Swim Team – Swim For Your Life" printed on the shirts to wear to Jimmy and Carolyn's Halloween party when we get home on Saturday night.

After all the morbidity at Alcatraz, I was ready for some "retail therapy", and suggested that we visit Union Square. Jim's overwhelming lack of enthusiasm didn't deter me from this side trip.

The stunning Dewey Monument sits in the center of Union Square. In 1903, it was dedicated as a tribute to the sailors of the US Navy commemorating the victory of the American fleet over Spanish forces at Manila Bay, the Philippines, in 1898, during the Spanish-American War. The 97-foot Corinthian column with a figure representing Victory at the top survived the 1906 earthquake.

Union Square is the central shopping district in San Francisco. This is a SHOPPING MECCA! It houses the largest collection of department stores and swank boutiques in the West including Macy's, Neiman Marcus, Saks Fifth Avenue, Tiffany & Co, Nordstrom's, Chanel, Louis Vuitton and many others. My pupils had completely dilated before my feet touched the sidewalk. As luck would have it (or was this strategic planning on Jim's part?), we arrived at 7:05 P.M. The stores all close at 7:00 P.M. All I could do was stand at the entrances and drool at the window displays. I could feel Jim breathe a sigh of relief at being spared from walking for hours through stores that did little to hold his interest.

Besides, it is cocktail hour and almost dinnertime!

Our last day in San Francisco was spent with Jim's brother, Jay and his wife, Joan. They graciously agreed to give us a first class tour that we would never have been able to do on our own. We rode down the serpentine Lombard Street. This is San Francisco's—and America's most crooked street. The steep, hilly street was created with sharp curves to switchback down the one-way hill past beautiful Victorian mansions. If not for the serpentine curves, easing out this treacherous slope, people would be killed rolling down.

Our tour continued down Fell Avenue (no relation), and through Haught Asbury which evokes images of the long-gone '60s hippie culture. Fragments of that flower-power, incense-burning, acid-dropping, tie-dyewearing,and peace-and-love era are still evident. We drove past the bank where the infamous Patty Hearst robbery occurred. That night we enjoyed a fine dinner at a local's restaurant under the Oakland Bay Bridge with a panoramic view of Alcatraz and the sunset in the background.

Our trip to San Francisco was coming to a close and we flew out to Reno, Nevada the next day. Jim rented an adorable little red convertible for our drive to Lake Tahoe. Unfortunately, we arrived on the same day as the first snowfall of the season, and were never able to take the top down. Coming from Florida, we were thrilled to drive in the mini-blizzard through the mountains to Lake Tahoe.

Our first gambling night was successful, having placed the roulette chips on our grandchildren's birthdays and won! Unfortunately, the blackjack dealers managed to get it all back the next night.

We were judges for the jack-o-lantern contest with entries from a local public school. The imaginations and creativity that went into carving the pumpkins was awesome. We wanted to vote for them all.

We took a day trip to Squaw Valley where the Winter Olympics were held years ago. The locals there were excited about the snowfall and were preparing for their winter season.

I treated myself to a world class facial at the onsite spa after 20 minutes in the sauna and an additional 20 minutes in the steam room then on to the beauty salon for a shampoo. I felt like a million dollars and floated up to our room.

The next day, on our drive back over the mountains to the airport, we were treated with another snowfall.

The trip home was uneventful with not a suspicious character in sight. We arrived in Ft. Walton beach after 9:00 p.m. and decided that we would convert our Halloween costumes into pajamas and climb into our own warm, cozy, soft, fluffy bed. We both agreed, coming back to our home here in Destin, truly is Paradise.

Did you ever wonder if baseball fans get the same enjoyment from an exciting baseball game as the players that are participating? Did you ever see a player stand up and sing, "Take Me Out to the Ballgame" during the seventh inning stretch? Maybe not, but I am sure this story will prove they both enjoy the same game equally, but in different ways. For both, it is a dream come true and you are invited to enjoy it with them, as Danny tells his story.

TAKE ME OUT TO THE BALLGAME

by Danny Fell (with introduction by James E Fell)

Pretend you are listening to an old fashion radio show;

The reader begins after the musical introduction, "CHARGE." As he starts to read, the baseball song "Take Me Out To the Ballgame" plays softly in the background.

THE SCRIPT;

Jack Norworth's 1908 classic "Take Me out to the Ball Game" was written on a scrap paper while on a train ride from Pittsburg to New York City. Norworth gave this scrap of paper with the lyrics to Albert Von Tilzer who composed the music and had it published. This is how the famous baseball song was born.

Although a baseball fan all these years, Norworth never attended a major league baseball game until June 27, 1940 when Major League Baseball presented him with a gold lifetime ball park pass on the 50th anniversary of baseball and the publication of his song, "Take Me Out To The Ball Game".

That day in 1940, the old Brooklyn Dodgers beat the Chicago Cubs five to four.

Now, 70 years later, do we still have baseball fans as loyal and as dedicated to the game as Jack Norworth? Do we still have fans that stand up during a seventh inning stretch, reach out and find that magic moment of hope? That hope is the very same magic that can turn a crowd noise into an unrehearsed roar that will shake the stadium with as little encouragement as a long foul ball.

Danny, is the youngest of five, and was only five years old when the family moved from St. Louis to Florida. Danny attended high school in Florida, then to journalism school at the University of Georgia and on to Atlanta where he now works in cable TV news. Through all those years Danny never stopped being a Cardinal baseball fan. His story becomes even more interesting when you discover this wasn't the first time he left Atlanta for the eight hour drive to St. Louis without so much as a prayer for getting a ticket to a World Series game. He just wanted to be near his team in their hour of glory.

In 2004, when the Cardinals were in the World Series with the Boston Red Sox, he drove the eight hours to St. Louis only to be disappointed when they lost in four straight games. Once again in 2006, he got the fever when St. Louis won the National League Championship and were ready to face the overwhelming favorite, Detroit Tigers.

Still recalling the 2004 Boston massacre….. Many sports writers were picking Detroit in five, Detroit in four, and one pompous Boston writer sarcastically picked Detroit in three. We don't know if that is what got him going this time, but nevertheless, he went.

Originally written as a thank you note to his brothers who helped him obtain a lifetime dream, a ticket to a World Series Game. Here is Danny's story.

SEVENTH INNING FEVER

by Danny Fell

There were certain moments in my life when the dreams of my youth ran head first into the responsibilities of my adulthood. Like the first time I priced my dream car, or the time my Ivy League aspirations saw my SAT scores. What usually followed was the slow, but certain, acceptance of those moments of compromise as just part of life.

However, when it comes to sports, these lines tend to get a little blurred. I grew up playing, watching, reading, collecting, or idolizing something sports related. As people get older their priorities change, and with that so does their passion for the games they admired as kids. But that's the thing with me, my passion did not go away, it just changed. Sometimes for the better; sometimes for the worse.

It was this particular crossroad where I found myself halfway into my trip to St. Louis. I was headed there with only the hope of experiencing a World Series celebration for my beloved Cardinals. It had been 24 long years since the last one, and I was only 8 years old then. So if it was going to happen this go around, I wanted something a little more tangible than the fuzzy memories of a small child, I wanted to be in the thick of it. I wanted to be one of those idiots you see in the streets or on TV after the game, but just the happy kind, not the handcuffed and tasered kind.

Which brings me back to the crossroad I mentioned. Halfway through my solo eight hour drive, my brain started working overtime. Even as I made my way through the beautiful Appalachian Mountains, I couldn't help but think, "why am I doing this?" I mean, I knew why I was doing it, but what was the point of it all?

Bam … There it was, adulthood trying to beat down my inner childhood. OK, maybe that's a little melodramatic, but the fact was, the thought got into my head and I knew it wasn't leaving anytime soon. All those rational thoughts I had repressed over the years were now knocking on the door of my adult conscience asking the hard questions. Why do I care so much about sports? Why do I spend so much time watching and reading about a bunch of spoiled athletes? Why do I spend so much money on the clothes, the memorabilia? And the kicker, does it really matter who wins or loses?

Arguments can be made for and against each of these points, but what really bugged me was the thought that, in the end, none of it would matter. That none of this could ever live up to the lifetime of expectations I had built up in my head.

But, when I arrived at my sister's house in St. Louis, I was still excited about the Series. How could I not be, the good guys were up two games to one. Nonetheless, those annoying nostalgia-killing thoughts would not leave my head. To make matters worse, that night's game was rained out, giving me more time to stew on this. So what did I do? I went searching for tickets on the web, of course.

To my surprise I found one "reasonably" priced ticket. After some convincing from my brothers and father, we decided this was an experience I shouldn't pass up., i.e.: they would agree to pay for it. Thanks again Guys. They said I would be representing the family, which meant, now I had guilt to go along with my crisis of sports conscience.

When I got to the game, I was both equally psyched and apprehensive. Psyched about being at an event I had always dreamed about and apprehensive that the lifetime of hype would crush the moment. I figured if my fears had any validity they were about to get the ultimate test. So what happened the moment I sat down? The Tigers hit a homerun! I swear on the Stan Musial Statue, the moment my ass hit the seat, Sean Casey's long fly ball cleared the fence. Mind you, I was by myself and at that point I was pretty sure everyone around me was convinced I was somehow related to the famous Billy goat that haunts our friends in Wrigleyville.

Thankfully, as the night grew older and the wet weather settled down, so did the home team. My Cards chipped away at a 3-0 deficit with single runs in the third and fourth innings. Then in the seventh, my apprehension started to fade away into the misty air. It started with a catchable David Eckstein drive that Detroit's Centerfielder turned into a slip-and-fall double. Then when the Cards tried to move their good luck charm over to third with a sacrifice bunt, the Tigers added to their how-not-to-field highlight reel when their pitcher air mailed the free out over first base, tying the game at three. This was their sixth error of the series and fourth by their pitching staff, giving them a new record.

Normally this type of baseball isn't all that exciting, but as I happily found out, all game changing moments are exciting when you are at the World Series. Especially when it gives new life to your team.

A few moments and two outs later, Preston Wilson delivered an RBI single to finally give the Redbirds a four to three lead! The place was going nuts and I was enjoying that rare and awkward moment that only happens at sporting events – high five-ing a group of complete strangers.

Unfortunately, the Tigers came right back and tied the game up in their half of the eighth. In years past, because of the way T.V. amps up the broadcasts for playoff baseball (i.e. cut-always to the saddest sacks in the stadium), I would have been overrun by feelings of doom and gloom right about now had I been watching TV, but it never got like that in the stadium. The place still had that buzz from the inning before. It was like they knew this was just something to add to the excitement of an inevitable win. And it also helped that Joe Sad Sack was no where to be found in my section of the upper deck.

Our boys were able to limit the damage to just that one run and took this see-saw game into the bottom of the eighth, all knotted up at four. There they faced Detroit's nasty reliever, Joel Zumaya, and his blistering fastball. After your "standard" sequence of a walk, fielder's choice, strikeout, and passed ball, the home team had a man on second with two outs. And in a game full of twists and dramatic turns, it was only fitting that the man coming to bat would be the same man in the middle of most of the action during this memorable night – David Eckstein.

On paper, seeing a 5'7" Shortstop step in against the 6'3", 210 pound fire-baller with a Hells Angel's goatee and a *flame tattoo* streaking down his throwing arm – well you can't help but think "that's just not fair," but this isn't on paper. It's the World Series, and after watching four consecutive ninety nine mph fastballs blow by him, Eck took a mighty swing at a high and tight fastball and drove it into the left-centerfield gap. It hung in the air for what seemed like eternity, and when Detroit's speedy left fielder, Craig Monroe, laid completely out for the ball, I swear you could hear a collective gasp from the crowd. Fully extended, the ball appeared headed for one of the better catches in World Series history. At the last possible second, it glanced off the webbing and landed for a go ahead RBI Double.

At that moment, the whole stadium just erupted. I swear, unless you are a structural engineer, feeling a stadium with 46,470 people physically shake from the cheering may be one of the coolest things you can ever experience.

With that type of build up, only an idiot would detail a story like this if the home team ended up losing. I'm no idiot. The good guys sealed the victory with a 1-2-3 ninth to move one step closer to the ultimate prize. As I followed the throngs of overjoyed Redbird fans out of the stadium that buzz in the air I felt earlier was now everywhere. The home team was up three games to one, but unlike the series in '1967 or the '"Royal disaster" in 1985, this one was different. This one seemed inevitable. You could see it in the smiles where the adults looked like kids and the kids looked like lottery winners.

What a way to make my inaugural visit to the newest entry in the Busch Stadium family. Busch No. III was so nice in fact, that once I got outside, I decided to make a u-turn back into the stadium just to savor the moment some more. While I stood there, in the now nearly empty stadium, I realized most of my fears had been erased during this unforgettable night. The moment did live up to the hype.

Unfortunately, I still had the one lingering thought – If my guys were able to close things out and bring home that championship, "what would be the point of it all?" Would it be just another cool moment or would a lifetime of anticipation have something more meaningful to show for it?

When game five arrived, I knew I had to be in a lively environment close to the action. So my sister and I headed downtown to watch the game at Paddy-O's – an outside bar literally just outside of the stadium. As much fun as I had being at the game the night before, in some ways this was better. Even though, it was crowded and hard to see the big screen TV's at times, the place had this awesome communal feel, I mean it's not often you can jam a bunch of people in a cold tented area, and feed them overpriced beer all night, and *still* have everyone happily united for the same cause. Needless to say the atmosphere was electric.

Unlike the night before, this game was more of your typical low scoring affair. There were a couple early lead changes, but outside of a home run and Detroit's nightly Pitcher throwing error, the drama was much more condensed. And in this case, once the Cardinals took three to two lead in the fourth inning, it all centered on them holding on to that lead. The great thing about this was, once they reached the seventh inning, the countdown was on. Every time an out was recorded, the whole bar would recite how many were left like it was a long drawn out New Years countdown. And what really made this part great was that it never felt like false hope. Like the night before, it was in the air. Not if, but when!

And so it came down to the top of the ninth with the home team needing only three more outs until the best fans in the baseball could erupt in mass celebration. The whole place was glued to each one of young Adam Wainwright's pitches, as he tried to continue his epic October run. Thrust into the closer role just a month prior due to an injury to fan favorite Jason Isringhausen, Wainwright was looking to close out his third straight playoff series. The rookie hurler did his best izzy impersonation by being dominant and dramatic at the same time. First batter – strike out! TWO OUTS TO GO! Second batter – base hit. Third batter – strike out! ONE MORE TO GO! -six pitch walk.

Now with two on and two out, in stepped Brandon Inge and his twenty eight regular season home runs. But, like the night before, Wainwright showed some of that bulldog-like resolve he obviously picked up from his mentor. The first pitch got Inge swinging and missing. The crowd erupted! Second pitch – Wainwright gets him watching strike two. Our area was going crazy and you could *still* hear the roar from the stadium behind us.

So now it all comes to one more strike. One more out. And Wainwright didn't waste any time throwing a wicked 94 MPH slider to get Inge flailing at strike three. We didn't really see what happened next because the place just exploded. Everyone was jumping up and down! Beer was strewn about in place of celebratory champagne!

The whole feeling was totally amazing! It was like it was straight out of the movies. Bands immediately started playing music on the street corners. People spilled out in the streets in the thousands. Downtown became an instant party. Car horns never sounded so good! And once again the phenomenon of strangers high five-ing each other became the norm.

After enjoying this for a while, I stepped back and looked around, letting it all soak in. What I saw was something truly special. I saw peoples' lucky shirts and hats transform into personal trophies. I saw a brand new stadium instantly become a timeless landmark. And I saw brothers and sisters, mothers and daughters, sons and fathers, and a whole bunch of friends; share a special moment that no one can ever take away from them.

But most importantly, I saw these moments become so much more. They became unforgettable memories that so many people will cherish for the rest of their lives. And for many of these people, these memories will give them a sense of pride for their home town and remind them how great things can be when we are able to come together and truly enjoy life.

So as I stood there in the street enjoying *my moment,* I realized everything *did* live up to my expectations. And while it may not have solved the world's problems, in the end, it really *did* matter. And I will forever have these memories to remind me.

(Thanks again guys!)

GO CARDS

If you have ever been on a flight with a crying child, you will enjoy the silence as Nancy tells her story, and don't miss the text message she sends to her sister in law, the mother of the crying baby, at the end of the journey.

CRIES IN THE SKIES

by Nancy Murphy

When Aunt Angie and Uncle Dave got married in St. Louis, Auntie Carolyn and Uncle Jimmy made the trip with their fourteen month old, Christina, in her car seat for the fifteen hour drive. This was before videos and DVD players in cars, so music and parental attention was the only entertainment for the little strapped in traveler. Aunt Nancy took a flight to St. Louis, because she had to be back to work right after the wedding.

Sunday morning after the wedding, Auntie Carolyn, with her ever-so-convincing logic, developed a plan to let Christina join her Aunt Nancy on the flight home, saying the baby wasn't feeling well, had cried most of the trip, and was miserable. With Aunt Nancy, she will be home in two hours and won't even know how it happened! So, that was the story we WERE to tell Christina when she got older about her very first plane ride... Unfortunately, Christina, being only a year old, was not used to being separated from her mom or dad for very long. No sooner than Aunt Nancy took Christina onto the airplane she realized something was not right, as Christina began a meltdown. Her crying started before the plane took off and continued non-stop for two hours and fifteen minutes, until the plane landed in Tampa. Thank God for pre-9/11. Back then, passengers just got annoyed and would ask to change seats, but today, they most likely would have turned the plane around and asked the offending parties, not so politely, to depart the plane!!! Fortunately, for her beauty and sweet pathetic cry, the flight attendant and the passenger seated besides Aunt Nancy, did their best to try to calm and entertain this sad little angel. The man sitting next to her, opened his brief case and desperately tried to find anything to make her smile or laugh like his business cards, his watch, his calculator, his pens, and whatever he could find that could somehow simulate" but to no avail. Finally, about an hour and half into the flight, she fell asleep, but still heaved as if she was still crying while sleeping. When the flight landed, Aunt Nancy and the baby exited the plane with stares and glares, but also a few nice empathetic goodbyes, from others who had experienced a similar flight with their young ones at some point in time. Christina wasn't one hundred yards off the plane, when Christina's grandmother, Meema Paradise, and her Auntie Jean whisked her into their arms and off to her home in Lakeland.

Before leaving the airport Aunt Nancy sent the following text message to the parents; "Ground control to Uncle Jimmy and Auntie Carolyn … the crying eaglet has landed and has been delivered safely to her nest."

Mattie Grace Pierce is the ten year old daughter of a former Ole Miss football player and a beautiful blonde Southern lady we affectionately call, "Hot Momma". This story is a fine example of what a Jr. Southern Belle thinks about before her teen age years kick in and the hormones take over.

ANNABELL OF THE FAIRIES

by Mattie Grace Pierce

I was born in 2000, a, "millennium baby" you might say.
I was also known as "the almost Easter baby".
You know what's really cool?
My grandmother and my great aunt have the same birthday as me,
April 7.
Also, I have the same name as my great grandmother.
Now I don't seem so out of the ordinary.
So you might call me stuck in the middle.
I'm the weirdest kid I know.
Isn't that odd
Have you ever said that?
I, myself, am very confused.
For some reason I keep seeing tiny people at night around 12:00 a.m.
I think I should find out what it is.
Oh yeah, I forgot to mention my name is Annabelle McGruter,
10 years old, (almost eleven, yay! Finally!).

This is a story by and about the mother of Mattie Grace Pierce, AKA Annabelle McGruter. As for her mother's story, the title says it all.

BLONDES WITH GUNS

by Donna Pierce

I would like to preface my story with a short side bar. One of my favorite sisters-in-law, Tanya, is also my hunting buddy. Since this story was written, both Tanya and I have become accomplished deer hunters, but it didn't start out that way. We both were, at best, novice hunters, married to avid deer hunters, blonde and flat out dangerous.

It was all Tanya's fault. She was having the best time, always going hunting with the boys. I couldn't stand it because according to her, I was missing something big. So I started tagging along with my husband, Big Daddy, and he began to show me how it was done.

This particular day, Tanya and I were driving seventy miles north to meet Big Daddy and the rest of the boys for some big time deer hunting. Big Daddy called us on our cell phone and said it was too wet at our regular hunting camp and the boys had decided we should move across the state to another hunting camp that a friend owned. The trip would have taken over two hours. Daylight was burning and from our point of view, these two lady hunters were already about an hour late for a date with a big buck deer. We both felt this would be our day.

When we got to the camp, the boys loaded the gear in our car and they all got into one truck. Tanya and I would drive in my car, which was great. We had time to swap a few embellished girl stories and trade barbs about the boys. We realized when we turned onto the interstate that we were only twenty minutes from our old hunting camp, but two hours from where the boys were headed, so we called them on their cell phone and had them to pull over. We told them we had decided to go back to our first camp alone and that they should continue on to the other side of the state. We stopped, gave them their guns, wished them luck, and kissed them all goodbye. We were now flying solo, off to our very first hunting adventure alone. There would be no one to tell us what to do, where to hunt, or how to get there. We were so excited, you might even say exhilarated.

At the camp, we changed into our hunting outfits and got our guns out to go over the loading thing. We did have a little trouble trying to remember how to load one of the guns, but we managed. This would be a day of many firsts, our first time of hunting with no men along, having to load the guns by ourselves, and making sure we had everything we needed for the next three or four hours. But our biggest first was the transportation to the deer stand. Big Daddy and the guys always drive those big ugly camouflaged four wheelers, but for getting around the base camp we had this cute little gas powered golf cart that had been completely covered in camouflage paint just like the big four wheelers. This beautiful new toy had never been used to hunt and we were about to use it. At this point in my story I should remind you once again, Tanya and I are both blondes. With that said, let the adventure begin!

As we checked out the area where we wanted to hunt, we received some unsolicited help in the way of advice from a group of fellow male hunters. I think all they really wanted was to make sure we were no where near them or a deer. After we figured out where we wanted to hunt, we loaded our golf cart with our gun cases neatly packed with ammunition, water bottles, lipstick, blush and some snacks.

So over the river and through the woods, we began our journey. We talked about how we would bag a huge deer and make our men proud of us. We even decided it might be a good idea to give them a little credit for having taught us so well. As we approached the area we had selected for the hunt, we crossed this precious old wooden bridge, made a quick left turn and came to a sudden stop. Out in front of us was a huge ugly gumbo of a mud hole. We paused to take it all in, but decided we had only one option and that was to shoot right up the middle following the tracks of all those other hunters that had gone before us. So we did. And guess what happened … We got stuck! The mud and water was up to the axle on the golf cart. After water crept up over the floor board and onto our designer boots, we stopped laughing and stepped down to survey the situation into knee-deep mud.

We decided I would give the cart gas and Tanya would push. We tried that and all we managed to do was sink the cart a little deeper. I got out and we both pushed and pulled and pushed and pulled, to no avail. We rounded up large tree branches and shoved them under the tires and pushed and pulled some more. It was a crisp fall afternoon, but Tanya and I had sweat soaking up every part of our hunting outfits that were not already covered with mud. My mother once told me Southern girls don't sweat - they glisten, but we discovered when two blondes were alone in the woods and stuck in the mud, they not only sweat - they cuss.

Needless to say, our hair was no longer blonde and beautiful and our makeup was a mess. We stopped to rest and survey the situation once again. It was then we remembered that one of our fellow hunters had left his four-wheeler down a turn row to the right of the bridge. We decided to go get it and pull ourselves out with his four-wheeler. We began the quarter mile walk but our new boots were so heavy from all the mud inside them; we were exhausted when we finally reached the four-wheeler. When a woman exits a vehicle in the woods, she leaves her keys in the ignition, but our male friend didn't. He most likely had them in his pocket and was up in a tree stand somewhere in Mississippi.

Tired, sweaty and disheartened, we walked back to the mud hole and told each other that come hell or high water, we had to get this vehicle out of this mud before any of the hunters made it back. We would never live this down if any one of them drove up and saw this. So we pushed and pulled again and, again, but failed to budge the cart. While walking around the front of the cart, to our surprise, we found our golf cart had a winch! For those of you who don't know what a winch is, it is a motorized piece of equipment that has a steel cable you can attach around a tree or something sturdy and let the winch pull you out of the mud. In less than five minutes we were free. We decided not to go back the way we came. Instead, we went the opposite way, giggling and laughing all the way. That is, until we drove right under a tree stand with two very unhappy male hunters frowning down at us. We should have apologized, but all we could think about were those stories that would be told for years to come, about the time they were drawing a bead on a big buck deer, and two blondes drove up in a camouflaged gas powered golf cart, yada, yada, yada…

Without a word said, we quickly turned our golf cart around and with no other options available, simply smiled, waved, and headed back in the direction of the mud hole. As we approached the mud hole from hell, Tanya discovered we also had a four-wheel drive button on our golf cart that should take us through almost anything. Tanya hit the button, I hit the gas, and we went straight through that mud hole without even slowing down.

We finally made it to our deer stand. There we sat, guns loaded and waiting, but every time we looked at each other, we would start laughing again only this time, as quietly as possible. Tanya said, “if the boys had been watching us, they would have peed in their pants laughing,” but swore we would never tell them. After two hours and no deer in sight, we just sat there and wondered if maybe, deer really could smell perfume.

We did not let this little adventure discourage us. We even told the boys the whole story and went on to become well respected hunters on our own. That hasn’t stopped the boys from telling stories about Tanya and me shopping around for some camouflage lipstick and odorless perfume.

Tired of the usual, politically correct, Christmas cards companies send out to their clients? One Christmas I decided to do something a little different in our firm with my "Snowbird Heaven" card. We got a lot of sincere feed back from clients who appreciated the originality and the effort. Apparently one of them even sent it to the local newspaper where it was published with full credit given to "Anonymous".

THE NIGHT BEFORE CHRISTMAS IN SNOWBIRD HAVEN

by Santa

T'was the night before Christmas,
And Santa was cranky
He flew through the snow
To find every Yankee.

His suit was a mess cause
Their chimneys were small,
And the air was so frigid
His reindeer would stall.

On Dancer, on Prancer
Let's get away from this sleet.
Just head for Florida,
We'll find us some heat.

Over the swamps and
Down the coast,
They dropped off their gifts
And were warm as toast.

He turned at the Keys,
then up the Gulf Coast they flew,
Just one last stop,
They soon would be through.

He circled over Destin
To admire the scene,
Sands of white and water,
Emerald green.

He yelled to Rudolph,
something must be wrong.
This town's one mile wide,
And thirty miles long.

Never-the-less, he
Finished his work,
And with the last toy,
He turned with a jerk.

As the sun pushed up
On the Eastern sky,
Santa smiled to his team,
And said with a sigh,

"This place is nice,
It's warm and sunny.
I have an idea
That's sweet as honey."

"For a thousand years,
We have worked every day,
And get no pay."

"Now look around here,
And what do you see
Green grass for you
And beaches for me."

"You surely know what
I have on my mind,
A place to live
Where the weather is kind."

"So let's get started,
And have no fear,

Now we will go north, but one day a year."

Then I heard him exclaim
As he turned in for the night
"Merry Christmas, Ya'll, and ya'll have a good night."

Ya hear?

A few years ago I decided to write a family history and give it to my children for Christmas. Shortly after I started the research, I found I had bitten off far more than I could possibly chew. In self defense I wrote this apologetic explanation telling my children and grandchildren why their family history was unfit to be put in a family tree without starting a forest fire.

TO THE BEST OF MY KNOWLEDGE

by James E Fell

Dear, Kids

This story started out to be one of those family histories, with all the tree limbs, family branches, and even a bad apple or two, but the more I got into it, the more I realized I knew precious little about the genealogy of both families. Besides, all that stuff with old English names and who begot who is pretty boring. Not really knowing what I was going to do, I started with some research. Well, at least I started by writing your uncle Bud to get the dirt on the Scanlon and the Duggan families on your mother's side, and to drop an e-mail to my sister in St. Louis to find out about the Fells, the Barefoots, and the Daniel Boone stories, on my side.

I intended for this family history to be a Christmas present to you children, just like the one last year when I wrote each of you a little book of short stories, about all the funny and nasty little things you did when you were kids. It wasn't until our Thanksgiving trip to north Georgia for a family reunion, that Angie gave me the package from Uncle Bud that made me realize, I had a problem. Now I had a complete history of the Scanlons and the Duggans along with pictures that told the bold truth about those rowdy Irish immigrants, warts and all. I thought just how good it made my side of the family look in comparison. Just as I was feeling a bit smug about my own heritage, I got home to find an e-mail response from my sister that made me want to change my name and move to China. I realized there was no way I *could* put all these stories and family secrets into one little family tree, without causing a forest fire. It needed some sort of explanation. How would I ever look my grand children in the eye again? I knew I had opened a real can of worms.

I lay in bed at night thinking that maybe I will just write it all down and put it in a safety deposit box somewhere to be read aloud long after I have departed. Then, on second thought, as much as I like to write, I could never make up stuff this good, and even if I did, no one would ever believe it. So if I just tell the story in book form, almost like I had gotten it directly from those formerly reliable relatives, it just might work. Maybe then you kids and the grandkids would feel some serious guilt about considering a Baker Act for dear old Papa.

Just for the record, to say I didn't embellish or make anything up, may not be totally true. But then, I have included the original letters from your Uncle Bud along with the e-mail from my sister. I offer these documents to prove to you that at least most of the things I have told you in this story if not historically correct… may be as close to the real truth as you will ever get.

Love, Dad

As children often do, ours were always asking questions about how their mother and I met and who their ancestors were. Although they had heard bits and pieces of the stories along with gossip from aunts, uncles, and cousins, I thought it was time to put it all together. A family history was the perfect place to show them where they came from. Little did I know how many people I would anger.

IRISH IS AS IRISH DOES

by James E. Fell

Your mama's maiden name was Dale, but that was only because the Scanlon and Duggan boys liked the way your granddaddy Dale played baseball. When your grandmother Ida took her young fiancé to the family picnic to meet the Duggan's, he never knew he was really being tested. As a point of interest, that is the same way I got into the family, only by that time they had raised the bar a bit. I not only had to prove I could play baseball; I had to pretend I was Catholic, even though at that time, I was not.

It was like an annual tradition at the family picnics, that the Scanlon and the Duggan boys would challenge each other to a baseball game. Everyone knew what was going to happen but gathered around anyway, just to watch. About the fourth inning of every game there would be an argument followed a couple of plays later by a hard slide into second base and the fight would start. It was there that I learned, by the grace of Peggy's mother, I was a Scanlon, at least for the fourth inning of the family picnic softball game. The fight was never serious and was always followed by beer drinking and storytelling with never a word about who hit who first.

Although we have always referred to the St. Louis Irish clan as the Scanlons and the Duggans, it was by number mostly Scanlons. There was only one Scanlon-Duggan marriage that we know of and that was between your great Aunt Cecelia Scanlon and Lester W Duggan. Although behind in numbers, the Duggans did a good job of catch up, with their eight children and thirty-two grandchildren. This is not to say that the Scanlons and the Duggans never crossed paths in their history, both families had common talents and common interest in singing, the stage, and entertainment. They may very well have had ancestors that came over on the very same boat from Ireland, or they may have even acted in the same play, but we have no way of knowing if they ever did.

The Scanlon history we have goes back to the early 1800s when Cecelia Scanlon was born in Athens Greece on the way to America from Ireland. Now, students of geography may question that because they know the shortest distance between two points is usually a straight line, however for the sake of the story; just accept it as one of those unexplainable things. Nevertheless little Anne, as she would be known, was Irish by blood and Greek by birth. Her mother was Mary Anne Scanlon and although unrelated but with the same sir name, her father was Daniel Scanlon. They were your great, great, grandmother and grandfather. Their family settled in the South near Nashville, Tennessee. Anne had a brother Daniel, who was named after his father and was four years older than Anne. When their father was killed in a work-related accident, young Daniel took over and became the man of the family. Daniel was successful in business. He worked, married and financed his little sister Anne through college. Anne began a career as a singing actress and later earned the title, “Songbird of the South”.

My side of the family tree started in a small town in Oklahoma where, my dad, the construction worker and my mom, the singer, met and were married.

THE SINGER AND THE CONSTRUCTION WORKER

by James E. Fell

Your grandfather, who was my father, had grown up as an orphan. He and his brother, Leonard and sister, Ethel were placed in foster homes after their father left home and their mother became very ill. Their mother ended up in a TB sanatorium for the rest of her life, although it was later found she never had TB. My father, along with the other two Fell children, were placed on farms with foster parents near Des Moines, Iowa, while still in their early teens. Dad was a hard worker and very smart. The family he stayed with wanted to send him to college and on to medical school. In 1917, when dad was only 15 years old, an epidemic of influenza broke out throughout the world and millions died. One by one the people that took care of dad died of the flu, including their teen age son. Dad told me there were so many deaths the city could not take care of the bodies. One day a policeman came by the farm and told dad to dig a deep grave for the family and mark it so one day they could be moved to a proper grave. It was in the middle of a severe winter freeze and the ground was so hard my dad had to use a pick ax to dig the grave where he buried all three family members on their farm. At the tender age of fifteen, he picked up his brother and headed for Detroit to get a job. They had very little money, but got jobs as brick masons on a large hotel construction project by lying about their age and experience. Dad was good at watching and following experienced workers and stayed on, but his brother, Leonard, who did not like the work, was fired. Leonard found he had talent with a camera and went on to make photography his life's work. Dad stayed in construction and moved from city to city, following the work. He went from Detroit, to Chicago, to Miami, to Houston, or wherever there were bricks to be laid.

In 1929 his company sent him to a small town in Oklahoma to build a five story bank building. It would be the largest building in the town. He was now a superintendent making good money. One day he heard this lady singing on the local radio station and fell in love with the voice, then went to the radio station to meet her. A short time later they were married and were blessed with a Christmas present on December 26, 1931, my sister, your aunt Jerry. Her birth came shortly after the stock market crash and the young couple with a small baby were in the mist of the greatest depression the world had ever known... The bank building my dad was constructing was just up to the third floor of the planned five, but out of money. The owners shut the job down and didn't finish it until 1940, eight years later. Now with no job and little hope they found out another baby was on the way, me. Dad's company told him to shut down the bank job and move to Manhattan, Kansas to finish up a project there, but after that, they told him they would have no more new work. They moved to Kansas and on December 14th, 1932, in the middle of a snow storm, I was born. With no job, a one year old baby, a two week old baby, and very little money they headed back to Oklahoma to seek work.

The years that followed were hard as the family moved back to Chickasha, Oklahoma to live with my grandmother Routh. Dad took the cash value from his life insurance to buy a candy route from a man who took his money but continued to sell other products on the same route to his old customers. Dad countered by developing his own line of homemade candies with his own recipes. Even as a very young boy, I can remember my parents picking up and shelling pecans by the thousands. His candies and his friendly personality won over the old customers and we made it through the eight years of the depression until construction started up again. My memories of those days are good ones, and although we had very few of the material things children today have, we were happy. Occasionally, I remember when there was not much food, but we always had something. When World War II started and construction was booming again, dad had good jobs building Army camps, Air Force bases, and factory buildings. I thought we were rich. I still remember the first time going to the store with my mom and buying almost anything we wanted.

Dad made many friends through his work during the war. After the war one of the friends asked dad to come to St. Louis and go into business building houses. They bought used Army trucks and equipment, all that was available after the war and then started building small subdivisions. After two years they parted friends and dad went back to what he knew best, the bricks. He started his own company as a masonry contractor. As a side line he would design and build a single home, we would live in it for a year or so and then sell it when our new home was finished. Dad and I built two of these homes, almost by ourselves. I was to learn more about construction from that first hand experience working with my dad, than all the other jobs and education that would follow.

When I returned from the Army, my brother Jay, who was born when I was a senior in high school, was nine. My dad had hurt his back and was confined to bed. The family needed someone to run the business and I was it. I actually went to work the same day I returned home. A year later when dad got out of bed and back to work, I had moved the company out of home building and into commercial construction. We were doing close to a million in sales and were preparing to start the masonry work on a 20 story hospital building.

While all this was going on, I met your mom, married and was looking forward to raising a family. Never in my wildest dream did I think our family would end up with three boys and two girls of our own plus, two boys and a girl we added as foster children. And just think it all started with a singer and a construction worker during the great depression, in a little town in Oklahoma.

If your great grandfather's name was BB Barefoot, wouldn't you think you were at least part Indian and entitled to an oil well in Oklahoma and some of those Native American perks? Well, I did and I WAS WRONG.

INDIAN CHIEF OR ENGLISH NOBLEMAN

by James E. Fell

For seventy years of my life, I have lived thinking my uncle, B. B. Barefoot was the son of a very important Chickasaw Indian Chief. My uncle, who was really my great uncle, was the Chief Justice of the Oklahoma Criminal Court of Appeals. He and my Aunt Mimi, really great aunt Mimi, lived directly across the street from the Oklahoma State Capitol building. That's the one with the working oil well in the front yard. Each summer my sister and I would spend a week with the Barefoots, but never the same week as Aunt Mimi wanted to devote her entire attention to teaching my sister the social graces. She would say she needed all her energy to watch over the mean little boy that managed to stomp on her flowers, chase her cat, and scare her gold fish by splashing their water to make waves. Every chance she got she passed me off to uncle Burt who would take me across the street to the state capital building, where I had the run of the place while he and governor Kerr, later senator Kerr and CEO of the Kerr-McGee Oil Company, would smoke big cigars and talk politics.

I feel sure it was the judge that planted that nasty lie about the Indian Chief, but as a six year old I didn't know he was only joking so I spread that lie for the next seventy years. It was not until a year ago that I saw the light. While having a family history lesson from my older sister, I learned the ugly truth. When it comes to family matters, my sister really knew how to dig the dirt. In one short conversation she burst all my family balloons. First of all, she informed me that Burt B. Barefoot was not my uncle; he was my mothers' uncle which made him my great uncle. He wasn't a Native American Indian, he was English and my aunt Mimi really did hate me. It was rumored she told someone I was, "a dirty little fish killer".

It was bad enough to find out the name Barefoot was not Indian, it was even worse to find out he was English. When I was investigating the Fell side of the family, I found that the Fell name was English as well. When I Googled the Fell name, once again I was directed to England and a very notorious Fell. The story of Jack the Ripper is well known as the first recorded serial killer in Europe, but few recall Jack was never caught. Oh, but there were suspects, and one such suspect fit the evidence that the Ripper was known to have great surgical skills, displayed in the manner the victims' bodies were mutilated. Doctor Fell, a London surgeon, was questioned extensively by Scotland Yard. It was common in England murder cases, that poems and stories about the prime suspects were published to keep the mystery alive. One such poem was titled "I Do Not Like Thee Dr. Fell" and went on, by innuendo, to suggest Dr. Fell was the surgeon known as Jack the Ripper. The only saving grace is that he was never convicted … but then neither was OJ.

To err is human, to keep it going for seventy years, is dumb.

WHAT ABOUT DANIEL BOONE

by James E. Fell

I remember my grandmother Routh well. I was her favorite and she always wanted me to stay with her at her house. She had a special feather bed that was just for me. She lived across the street from the First Methodist Church where she and I attended Sunday school, Sunday Church service and Wednesday night prayer service. She lived for politics as long as they were the Democratic Party type. She took me on the train to all the small towns near us to nail up political posters on every telephone pole in sight. It didn't matter who was running as long as they were Democrats we nailed up their posters. I remember many of the small towns were so small the train would not stop they would just slow down so Grandma Routh would jump off and catch me, but most of the time we both ended up falling down.

It was an adventure and on Election Day I would pick up the ballot box from the polls and carry them on my bike to the newspaper office where the votes were counted and reported. I would end up at Grandmother Routh's house listening to the radio for the results. I remember one Sunday morning listening to that same radio when I heard the announcement that the Japanese had bombed Pearl Harbor and World War II had started.

Granma Routh and I were especially close but I don't ever recall her speaking about either of her husbands. I knew all of her other secrets like the bottle of gin she kept behind the block of ice in her ice box. Back in those days an ice wagon would come by each neighborhood and the man would bring a 50 pound block of ice and put it into a compartment like the ones where our modern freezer and ice trays are kept. Each time he came to grandma's, I would get her gin bottle out of the ice box and hold it until he got the new block of ice in, then I would carefully hide it behind the block of ice and we both would pretend I didn't know it was there.

I was shocked years later to find out her first husband had not been killed in a train wreck as we had been told, but had simply walked away from his wife and seven children. I also found out Frank Routh, her second husband, did not want the children around and the girls, including my mother, and the others were sent to live with an aunt in the same town where their mother and new husband lived. There was never much talk about what happened to husband number two, but my sister said Aunt Lola told her he had committed suicide.

Now, about that Daniel Boone thing. It seems grandma Routh's maiden name was Boone with traces of heritage in Virginia and Kentucky where Daniel Boone was born and raised. One of my mother's sisters did considerable research on the topic, even going to Virginia and Kentucky looking up names and tracing them to graveyards. She supposedly had the proof and it was fully documented, but on her return to Chicago she left the book with all the facts in the back of a taxi never to be seen again.

The four girls and three boys in Grandma Routh's family produced a slew of cousins for us and there was one of about every kind, style and character. One of my cousins ended up as an outstanding trial lawyer in Texas. Then there was his brother, who built an empire of dry good stores in Texas and was a millionaire before he was thirty five, but was unable to enjoy it much. He went to jail for drug trafficking. Another cousin ended up as a shock jock on the radio and was so obnoxious no one in the family wanted to admit we were related. We had a University of Alabama cheer leader who had a sister who was a card carrying Communist and suspected Russian spy. But, in the long run, we had more good than bad and who knows what they are saying about me. My favorites were my Uncle Dwight and Aunt Lola who never had children, so my sister and I got first class treatment when we visited them in Oklahoma City. They loved to travel and went to the Kentucky Derby every year. My uncle would go into the men's room right before the derby race and listen to the guys talking about the horse that didn't have a chance, then he would place a bet on that horse plus another bet on the favorite. He almost always won a lot of money.

Your mother was a wonderful woman and she left us at such an early age, I always feared you might forget her. I will never forget the funeral mass when we turned to leave the church and to see there was not an empty seat on either side of the isle. It was a fitting tribute to a woman who had devoted her life to motherhood, family and friends.

YOUR MOM

by James E. Fell

Your mother and her two cousins Ann and Helen Girst were inseparable. They went to school together, worked together and vacationed together. Growing up without a father was hard on the Dale children and even harder on their mother, Ida, but like all Scanlon woman they survived. When your mom graduated from school she had a job, but no way to get there other than the city bus which refused to wait for her when she overslept. In true Scanlon form, she took her first pay check and bought a car even though she had no idea how to drive. Her sister had married Jack Brandle and Peggy talked him into showing her how to drive around the church parking lot then each day she would simply wait for the city bus to come by and follow it to work until after a few trips she felt comfortable enough to go it alone.

I had just returned home from the service and was ready to start a family and get on with my life but I had a problem, no wife. All the girls I knew before I left home were married and some even divorced and married again. My brother-in-law, Bill Lenox felt sorry for me and told me there was a cute girl working in the office next to his by the name of Peggy and he would fix me up. When I called her she said her family was in the midst of moving from their house across the street from Sportsman Park, the old Cardinal baseball field to a home in Pine Lawn near the Girst family. Each time I called the move seemed to get in the way so we never got past an occasional phone call. In the mean time I met another girl and started dating her, but still calling Peggy now and then to see how the move was going. Later I found out it was really not the move that was putting me off, it was breaking up with her old boy friend Don Grimes. I was getting discouraged and would most likely never have called again except for one Freudian slip of the tongue. One day after work I called the other girl I had been dating and mistakenly called her Peggy. She hung up on me so I picked up the phone, called Peggy and got the date. It was May 3, 1957 and we were married May 3, 1958.

We both wanted a family right away, but went childless for six years. Doctor after doctor told us there was no reason we could not have children and we soon found out we could. We were pregnant. One day when Peggy was about seven months pregnant and was coming home from the store with groceries she found the men working on the street in front of our home had the driveway blocked. She had to park on the side street and walk through a neighbor's yard to get home. She tripped in the dark and hit her elbow on a concrete walk. When she came into the house she said she thought she had broken her arm. I looked at it and said, "No way, if it was broken it would be swollen". The next morning when we got up she said it still hurt. She didn't think she would be able to drive to the doctor for a regular baby check up and asked me to drive her. I sat in the waiting room and after about two hours she came out with a cast on her arm from her hand to her shoulder and a "I told you so" look for me. That night, although she swore it was an accident, she rolled over and smacked me in the head with her cast about five times.

About a week later she started having problems and I took her in to the hospital. The baby was coming early, but to our surprise and the doctors, it was **babies**, a little boy and a little girl. When the doctor came into the father's waiting room he said, "Well, you wanted a boy and you got one". "Peggy wanted a girl", I said, "but she will be happy with the boy". The doctor said, "She doesn't need to because you also have a girl. You have twins".

As happy as we were the doctors and nurses were cautious because of the very low premature birth weight. They said they might not make it, but if they could survive the first 48 hours the odds would go up. They made it to 48 hours and then the doctors said four days and when they made that mark, they said a week and you can take them home. Little Tracy, the boy, only made it to the sixth day and Stacy his sister died on day seven. After six years of waiting and then going from high to low put both of us in deep depression. Neither Peggy nor I could bear to attend the burial so my dad along with Bud Dale and Jack Brandle stood in for us. We were staying with the

Brandles and I knew I needed to get all the baby things out of our apartment before I brought your mom home.

I went back to work after a few days although still sad, I managed to get through the day, but I began to worry about your mom. She stayed in bed, spoke very little and ate even less. I knew I had to do something so I called around to all the agencies telling them we wanted to adopt a baby. They told me it would take months or maybe years and chances are we would be turned down because of our mixed religion and the fact that she still could have a child. As fate would have it, one day I heard on my car radio how great the need was for foster parents so I called. They sent a social worker to our home to interview us and she said if we got approved we would only be allowed to have small babies for short periods of time because of our mixed religion.

We left it at that and a few days later she called telling us they had an emergency and needed a family to take two small boys for a month or two. We expected babies and they showed up with two boys, one nine and one ten years old. Peggy called me at work and told me they were there and was I in for a surprise. I didn't know what the surprise was but at least she sounded happy for a change. As I drove home I thought these kids are most likely from a poor home and although we don't have much they will think we are rich. When I walked in the door I was met by Bobby, the youngest one, who proudly asked if I wanted him to make me a drink. "I can make a perfect Manhattan", he said. I realized he was serious and found later he had been trained to do this by his mom. His mother was the corporate auditor for all the Chrysler dealerships and had been taking bribes along the way. It was obvious by the questions they asked that the two boys had lived in the lap of luxury and we were the poor ones. The Child Care "month or two" lasted through high school, college and the Marine Corps. Bobby was killed shortly after his discharge in a motorcycle accident in Kansas City. I flew Peggy to his bedside just minutes before he died. It was here at the hospital in Kansas City where we met his mother who had gotten out of prison several years earlier, but didn't bother telling anyone until she got the call to come to the hospital. Peggy and I were grieving the loss of a son while his mother was busy finding out how she could collect the insurance money his company provided for accidental death. We took Bobby back to St. Louis where he was buried in the Scanlon grave plot near your grandmother Dale.

Once we got started having babies we couldn't stop. Those were the happy days, and some of the days I wrote to you about last Christmas. Those were just a few of the beautiful moments of our life when we could enjoy watching our children grow.

We watched as each of you grew up and became your own person full of all the tender care that came from your loving and devoted mother. Although small in stature like her great grandmother, Anne, she had the strength and courage to keep the family together, and above all to keep the family together.

The following group of stories may be considered a new twist on inviting someone over to watch your home movies but this one is a little different. I have taken some of the cute and nasty little things my children did while growing up and then fast forwarded 20 years to show you the cute and nasty little things their children did. which humorously proves, déjà vu really works.

THE CHILDHOOD ANTICS OF TWO GENERATIONS OR… WHAT GOES AROUND COMES AROUND

GENERATION # 1; (MY CHILDREN)

Nancy was our first baby, but you may remember her as the author of one of our first stories, "Cries In The Skies". This is a story about a little black and white hobby horse and a baby girl who loved to ride.

YAHOO, RIDE ' EM COWGIRL

by James E. Fell

For some reason I always thought every baby had to have a rocking hobby horse, so I bought Nancy one when she was about two years old. The horse was white with black trim and a black saddle. It was given a prominent position in our living room near the French doors leading out to the patio.

Nancy paid little attention to that little horse at first, but as she got older and her baby brother got interested, she did.. It was then she decided it was time to show us what she could do and he couldn't. She would get on the horse and rock so fast I thought she might go right through the wall next to the fireplace if something broke. To assure her safety and calm my wife down, I taught her to ride like a jockey with her feet standing in the stirrups above the saddle while whipping the horse's rump with her right hand. Then, I taught her to ride like a cowboy sitting back in the saddle and rocking back and forth shouting "Yahoo!", long before we even knew what a search engine was.

When friends, grandparents, or neighbors would come by to visit, I would put her through her paces on her hobby horse which made me very proud and happy, while her mother, her grandparents, and the neighbors were looking up the commitment instructions to Baker Act the baby girl's father.

As each new baby came into the picture they, along with other neighborhood kids, gave the hobby horse a try. Some rode fast and hard while others made a lot of noise. But none could ride like a jockey or yell "Yahoo" and ride like a cowboy. My baby girl retired as queen of the living room hobby horse at the tender age of four.

One thing for sure, when you have children, you will have at least one minor crisis each day, that at first may seem to be unresolvable, but in very short order, with a little help from mom or dad, they just go away.

DAD SAID IT WILL GROW BACK

by James E. Fell

With five children it was almost impossible for all to go to church at the same mass. I would normally go to church with Nancy and Jimmy while mom stayed home with the small ones and when we got back she would go.

I don't remember what happened that Sunday, but I do recall we were getting ready for our vacation to Colorado when I ended up going to church alone while Nancy and Jimmy stayed home with their mom to help pack.

The kids, most likely, know the details of what actually happened next better than I do. I remember coming into the house after church to find everyone crying. Nancy was crying uncontrollably. Jimmy was crying and at the same time, exclaiming "it wasn't his fault, it was an accident". Your mother was crying and holding this large beautiful lock of hair and telling me I had to get a doctor to put it back on. It wasn't until I could see the bald spot on top of Nancy's head that I realized where the lock of hair in her mother's hand belonged.

Angie had no clue what had happened, but started crying anyway. I grabbed the hair from mother and walked across the street to Dan Walker, a neighbor and our pediatrician. He just smiled when I told him the story and said, "Don't worry, it will grow back (a short pause) in about six months (Another short pause) … it may be a little different color, but (continuing to smile) she can always go blonde."

I went home a little despondent, but surprised to find everyone at home happy once again. The crying had stopped and her mother had already made her a new hair do that hid the bald spot. I was worn out but thought better of telling them all that the doctor had said so I just casually told them; "it's okay, he said it will all grow back… real soon."

This story has two lessons. The first is, that kids do listen to adults and are prone to repeat what they hear. The other is, be careful what you say, as you never know who is listening.

DAD TELL HIM I'M READY

by James E. Fell

No pun intended, but the truth is that my son, Jimmy Fell, fell in love at a very early age and as most first loves, his has never left him. Who was the lucky little girl? Well, no one, his first love was baseball and being in St. Louis, his favorite team was the St. Louis Cardinals. He not only loved the sport, he was very good at it. He was a natural and very competitive. He loved to win. Not a day would go by that he didn't have a bat or ball looking for someone to play with. If no other kids were around, he would throw the ball as high as he could, straight up and then stagger around until he got under it and made the catch.

When he reached little league age where they wore real uniforms, had actual coaches, and honest-to-goodness umpires in black shirts with face masks calling balls and strikes, he was in heaven. His good playing in the field and his batting did not go unnoticed. Many of the dads would congratulate him and jokingly say something like, "hey Jimmy, looks like you are about ready for the Cardinals."

His grandfather came up one summer from Florida to visit. We were at home watching the Cardinals on television, playing in Chicago. Jimmy knew the names of every player, his batting average, and even the statistics on the players on the bench who were not even playing. Jimmy's Granddad said, "Say, aren't the Cardinals coming home for a double-header this Sunday? How 'bout that Jimmy, would you like to go?" Did you ever see a six year old boy glow? I thought he would light up the family room as he asked, "Can we, can we Dad?" I told him I would see if we could get tickets, knowing full well several friends had season tickets and getting three or four tickets should be easy.

When Sunday came, my dad, Jimmy and my daughter Nancy, who was also a big fan, set off for the new Busch Stadium. We got there about two hours before game time, because Jimmy did not want to miss a thing. As a mater of fact, we were so early, that as we walked across the street from the parking garage to the main gate of the stadium, Jimmy kept hitting me on the leg and saying, "That's him, Dad, that's him, right there in front of us!" Well, "him" turned out to be Red Schoendienst, the Cardinal general manager. I looked down at Jimmy and said, "yes, I think it is Red." My dad joined in and confirmed that it was Red. Impatiently, Jimmy said, "Well tell him, and again, tell him Dad." I asked "Tell him what?" just as we were about to enter the main gate of the stadium. As loud as his little voice would carry he said, "Tell him I am ready!" My dad and I could not help but laugh out loud. Red Schoendienst, who must have heard every word, confirmed he had, with a big smile as he turned and reached down to shake Jimmy's hand. "I bet you are ready, son. Come and see me when you get out of school."

We all know moms have a special rapport with their children that is somehow akin to mind reading or ESP, but even then, at times, this emotional bond can go south. My advice to the fathers when this happens, is to do nothing. Trust me, they will work it out.

THE SPAGHETTI KID

by James E. Fell

When my first son, Jimmy, was very small, maybe just a year and a half old, I was able to talk to him and be understood even before he could talk back. Each day, when I got home, I helped his mom by changing diapers or giving him a bath, then getting him ready for bed. I knew he understood me. because I would tell him things like, how you should pick up his toys each night and put them in the toy box before he went to bed. With no further prompting, he would do it. When it came time to potty train him, his mom said she was having a hard time getting him to do anything and jokingly told me to go have one of my man-to-man talks with him. That night as I got him ready for bed, I explained how nice it would be if he used the potty and didn't have to wear diapers anymore. He said, "Okay" and I asked if he wanted to wear his big-boy pants to bed and he said, "Okay". This is the truth. He never wore a diaper again – he was potty trained!

One other night I was getting him ready for his bath and I noticed he had spaghetti all through his hair. I asked him how that happened and he got all excited and tried to tell me the story, but all I got was a few isolated words like "Mom, gettie boom!" then he would end up with both hands on the top of his head.

After I got him into bed, I went down to talk to his mom and told her the story and what I heard him say. I asked if she gave him spaghetti at lunch today and how it got in his hair. She calmly said, "It got there because I put it there. I fed him what he wanted, spaghetti, for lunch and he kept taking spoonfuls of spaghetti and throwing them against the walls. I cleaned it up told him that was not nice and even helped him eat with his spoon. Then he took two handfuls and threw them at me so I took the bowl and dumped it over his head." She said it, like she was glad she did it, and had no regrets. I felt as though I had just heard the confession of a schoolyard brawl.

That night, I decided my sweet loving wife and mother of my children, needed a short vacation, and I needed to stop those one-on-one conversations with my two year old son. Sometimes not knowing everything is okay, and better to just let them work things out their own way.

Want to be a hero? Take your daughters to lunch and be sure to tell the waiter "table for three, please".

TABLE FOR THREE PLEASE

by James E. Fell

As my girls grew up much faster than I wanted them to, my wife reminded me that my work was not nearly as important as my relationship with my two daughters, and especially Angie. She asked me what I was going to do about it, and I replied with the standard answer I had for every business problem, "I'll take them to lunch". Their mom said "Good idea. Tomorrow at 11:30 a.m. you pick them up. I will make reservations at Roncarrios." Now Roncarrios was the noonday Mecca for every construction guru in St. Louis. No one ever brought woman to lunch, especially ones as young as five and really cute. Their mom dressed them up, fixed their hair and when I walked in the restaurant, all eyes focused on these two beautiful little girls being escorted to their table by their father.

Instead of what I had expected to be jibs and jabs from my friends and business associates, I got nothing, but smiles and comments about my beautiful girlfriends. Most stopped by our table to give a special hello to the girls, and to thank me for reminding them that they needed to do the same for their children.

None of this seemed to bother my girls. They were just so proud to be dressed up and somewhere special with their dad. When it was over I took them back home. I got goodbye kisses and hugs from each one that made my day as special as theirs.

When Angie was the baby of the family, she was so loving and caring that we all referred to her as "Sweet Angie". That is, until we gave her two more brothers instead of a baby sister.

DAD THIS IS MY FRIEND

by James E. Fell

I am no psychologist, but my theory on the middle child syndrome, at least as Angie is concerned, is simple. As the family grew, and her brother Mike was born, she no longer was the baby of the family. Angie was convinced that Mike should have been a girl so she would have had someone to be a big sister, like Nancy was for her.

Trapped between two boys as immediate siblings she was lost in the middle. Her salvation came when she heard her mom was going to have another baby. This time it had to be a girl. The day I brought Danny home, I folded the little blue blanket back and said, "Angie, meet your new brother, Danny". She burst out in tears and literally cried for a week. That was the day we all said, "Goodbye to Sweet Angie".

When Angie finally decided it was useless fighting with her older sister, Nancy, she went out to find friends of her own, rather than fight over Nancy's friends. Angie made several close friends and invited them to our house to play, but never introducing them to her parents, her brothers, or her sister. Both her mom and I told her how it was proper to introduce your friends when you invite them to your home. For whatever reason that only Angie knows, she continued to bring new friends over, but deliberately not introducing them to us. Finally, I had enough and after her friend went home, I sat Angie down and scolded her for not obeying us and introducing her friends. From that day on Angie would bring a friend home and no matter what I was doing or how many times I had met that particular friend, she would interrupt and say, "This is my friend so-and-so." She would do it even if I had been introduced to her friend, so-and-so, twelve times before, or even if I was shaving, or taking a bath, or talking on the phone. This lasted all the way through high school although then, it was done with a big smile. It only ended when she got married to Dave and her friend, Lisa, came to St. Louis to be in her wedding. Lisa had practically lived with us in Lakeland and even worked for me as an architect for a short while. I got it one more time at the reception, when Angie laughingly said, “Dad, I want you to meet my friend Lisa.”

Every parent constantly sees things their children do that may be little clues as to what they will do when they grow up. Often we end up with a lot of confusion about the meaning, but this was not the case with Michael. After reading this story you will know what happened to Mike, but to know the rest of the story, you will need to read about his son Paxton in the second generation story called "Piano Player or Engineer."

LOOKS LIKE WE HAVE FOUND OURSELVES AN ENGINEER

by James E. Fell

When we left St. Louis, both Mike and Jimmy's grades at school had gone from perfect to perfectly bad. We had them both tested and a specialist said they were dyslexic and were going through a stage that they would most likely learn to control and manage, "Just like Einstein did." The walls of her office were covered with photos of doctors and well known, successful people, thanking her for her help. It was slow progress and as they each moved to higher grades in school, their grades slowly improved.

I didn't realize how smart Mike was until two events occurred in a single week, while he was in high school. The first was fostered by my frustration in keeping our swimming pool clean and free of algae. With five kids all going to a private school, extra money was hard to come by, but I finally broke down and paid $750.00 for a "Kreepie Krawley," an automatic pool vacuum that magically managed to sweep every square inch of my pool and turn that green mess into a vodka clear reservoir. I enjoyed just watching it do its thing. Mike watched too, but as I learned later, he had something else in mind. A few days later I came home to find my $750.00 Kreepie in 750 pieces, totally disassembled and laid out in perfect rows of screws and nuts across the concrete deck next to the pool. All Mike could say was "it wasn't working right" and he could not understand why I was upset since he knew how to fix it. Well, he did put it back together and it worked pretty well, but there were a few screws and things left over. His youthful explanation was that "they were not necessary."

A few days later, his mom and I were out for an evening walk and one of our neighbors stopped to talk. She was the wife of our family doctor and also the chemistry teacher at Mike's high school. She said, "Congratulation, your son, Mike just finished his chemistry class and scored the highest grades I have seen since I have been teaching at Santa Fe. I put two and two together and told my wife, "I think we have an engineer on our hands."

When I think of my son, Mike growing up in St. Louis, two things always come to mind, because they were not just one-time events like many of his adventures, they were almost daily events with just a twist or two in another direction. The first was his fascination with his "Big Wheels."

BIG WHEELS

by James E. Fell

Both, his buddy, John O'Neil, from next door, and Mike had a Big Wheel rider. This was one of those plastic toys that had one very large wheel up front and two smaller ones in the rear. The boys sat low between the two small wheels and controlled the big wheel with handle bars and foot petals. It was much like a low rider motorcycle for kids. The driveway between our two houses was very steep and ended with a stone retaining wall that prevented them from going over an eight foot embankment. There was room for a sharp right turn at the bottom of the driveway that would allow them to avoid hitting the wall.

Every day, like clockwork, they would run those Big Wheels side-by-side down the hill, faster and faster just barely making the right turn at the bottom. When they weren't running the driveway, they would just sit on their Big Wheels in the front of our house like a couple of cool bikers waiting for babes to walk by them on the sidewalk.

The second thing he did, was what gave him the nickname of, "The Money Man." A typical conversation between Mike and his mother would go something like this; His mother would say; "Come and go to the store with me, I need to get you some school clothes." Mike would reply; "I will go if you give me a dollar." Mom, "I'm not going to give you a dollar." Mike, "O.K., then 50 cents." Mom, "no way". Mike, "OK, but at least a quarter." Mom, "Here's a quarter, get in the car."

Unknown to us, Mike would take the quarter and buy the single wrapped penny candy and take it to school where he would sell it to his friends for a nickel each and turned his quarter into $1.25, for a 500% profit. This worked well for him right up until the time we received a “Cease and Desist” note from his teacher.

When you move to another state and into a new neighborhood it takes little boys just a few days to get to know all the people within two blocks in all directions along with their names, their kids names and their dogs.

DID YOU EVER SEE A DOG SMILE?

by James E. Fell

The early years in Danny's life were deeply influenced by two dogs. The first dog, Callie, was not even his. It sort of belonged to all the kids in the neighborhood. My first introduction to Callie came when I was telling Danny a bedtime story one night, soon after we had moved to Florida. After his story, Danny was telling me about a dog in our neighborhood that could smile. I told him dogs don't smile, but sometimes owners pull their mouth up at the corners and it may look like they smile, but it isn't. Dogs don't smile.

We had just moved into our new home in Lakeland and all the boys were checking out the neighbors, their kids and their dogs. By sundown, they knew all the neighbors within two blocks, along with the names of all the kids and their dogs. I was still in the kitchen unpacking from the move when I noticed a train of little boys would come in and out usually looking for something like a ball, a bat, or a fishing pole. The pecking order was Jimmy, then Michael, then one the neighbor kids that I didn't recognize, then our little Danny followed by Callie, the dog.

On one of these trips they all stopped near where I was unpacking dishes and Danny said, "Dad, this is Callie the dog I was telling you about that smiles." Without looking up, I said, "Danny, I told you dogs don't smile." Jimmy and Michael together said, "Well this one does." With that, they all said, "Smile Callie." I turned around to see this big mutt of a dog smiling from ear to ear. After a short silent period of "I told you so," one of the boys broke the silence and said they were going fishing. I asked where they would go, and the neighbor boy told me that they were going to the lake behind the orange grove. I told them "that was no lake, it was a sink hole, and there were no fish in there…but there might be alligators."

This time the dog led the way and they all followed her up the road toward the lake. There were no gators in that lake that I was aware of, but I thought it might help to keep them around home. A neighbor had told me the kids played up there often and it was safe.

About two hours later I heard the chatter of small boys and a barking dog coming up our driveway. This time I looked up in time to see the kitchen door open up and in single file, they came holding this fish as high as they could raise its head, almost above theirs, while the fish's tail dragged on the floor. They all gave me one more of those "I told you so" looks and their dog gave me another one of those big doggy smiles.

Stories about children and their dogs can make you laugh or make you cry. This one offers an abundance of both.

JUST ME AND THE DOG

by James E Fell

Danny's second dog was Sheba. One day two of the neighborhood kids and the dog, Callie, came by with a little brown puppy to show Danny, Jimmy and Michael. They knew I was easy, but the hard sell would be their mother. Their story was that, "if we didn't take the puppy, it would go to the dog pound and if no one took it home in thirty days, it would be murdered." Peggy told them no, as she reminded the boys that the last dog we had, everyone wanted, but she was the only one who took care of it. Poor little Danny, his voice holding back a cry, said, "I was too little to even remember that dog, but I promise I will take care of this one." Even Peggy could not resist the tear from her youngest and said, "Okay, but I want all three of you boys to sign a contract that no matter what, you will take care of that dog." They all signed the contract she wrote out on the back of an envelope and Sheba became a member of the Fell family. Little did we know at that time, how important that contract would become in our lives, especially the part where they promised, "no matter what, we will take care of our dog."

With the help of Callie (the smiling dog), who became Sheba's foster mother, and taught her all those things a dog must know to be a dog and one of the kids at the same time. The gang of little boys continued to come and go, but now the rear was brought up by Danny, Callie and a little puppy they named Sheba.

Years went by and Sheba grew to be a beautiful dog even bigger than Callie. She was a beautiful mix of collie and pit bull, with all the muscle of the pit bull, but the beautiful looks and color of a collie. While Callie was there, she was the leader, but one day Callie and her real owner moved away and Sheba took her well earned position as the queen dog of the neighborhood. In addition, she played outside left on the kid's soccer team, defensive back and free safety on the kid's football team, and retriever of lost baseballs when hit over a fence into a crabby neighbor's yard.

After Peggy's untimely death, Mike went off to the University of Florida in Gainesville. Danny and I stayed in Lakeland while Danny finished high school. When summer came, Nancy, Angie, Jimmy and his wife, Carolyn, all came to stay at our home in Lakeland. It was nice, once again, to have everyone around. I felt like we were still a family.

All good things come to an end and as summer turned to fall, Angie left for her senior year at Southwest Missouri State, Nancy moved to Winter Haven to be near her work, and Jimmy and Carolyn moved to Tampa, to be near his work. This left just the two boys and myself in that big house. Now that Danny was out of high school he had planned to go to Gainesville with Mike to attend the Junior College there while Mike started engineering school at the University of Florida.

The three of us were eating breakfast one day in August and I was saying how I dreaded the first of September when they would be heading up to Gainesville. I would be left here all alone, "just me and the dog." Some uncomfortable silence was followed by Danny clearing his throat and saying, "Well, Dad, we are leaving tomorrow to get an early start registering and all." Another moment of silence, then Danny continued, "And Dad … we're taking the dog with us."

A short time later I listed the house for sale and sold it to the first person who made an offer, then moved into an apartment. I visited the boys in Gainesville when I could and was surprised to see how well they had trained Sheba to do new tricks. They taught her to bite on a towel they had tied to the handle of the refrigerator and bring them a can of Bud Light while they watched TV, just like the dog in the television commercial.

The next year Sheba, now getting very high in dog years, went with Danny to Athens, Georgia where he had transferred to the University of Georgia while Michael stayed on in Gainesville to concentrate on his engineering degree.

As the years went on Sheba developed cataracts in both eyes and had painful arthritis that came from trying to support that large Pit Bull body on that German Shepherd frame. When Danny brought her home for the summer, we took her to our former neighbor, close friend, and veterinarian, to be checked out. He said to just give her a couple of aspirins with her food each morning and continue with the same love and care Danny has always given her and she would be fine. As we were leaving, he ended by saying, “Sheba will let you know when it is time.”

Shortly after Danny returned to Athens, I got a call. Danny could hardly talk. He was crying as he told me “it was time” and although he had to put Sheba down, he just could not bring himself to do it. I arranged to have a veterinarian service in Athens come by and make the necessary arrangements. This allowed Sheba to move on with the dignity and grace that our special friend and “Queen Dog of the neighborhood” deserved.

Several years later at Danny’s wedding I was asked to move his car. When I looked at his key chain, I saw a dog tag I immediately recognized with the name, “Sheba.” It was then that I finally realized, all the conditions in the contract that Danny and his brothers had signed, so long ago with their mother, had been fulfilled.

GENERATION # 2; (THEIR CHILDREN)

Remember the Spaghetti Kid. This story is about his first born son, who he named after his brother Mike but we call him Mikey

TRIP TO ST. LOUIS WITH PAPA

by James E. Fell

When little Mike was only five, he and Papa Fell set out for St. Louis to visit his cousins, aunt Angie, and uncle Dave. It all started out well as Papa Jim picked Mike up at his school, buckled him in his car seat right behind the driver and headed off to St. Louis. Papa Jim learned very quickly that little Mike, even though buckled tightly in his car seat, took but a few minutes to figure out how to operate all the switches, locks, lights, and the small portable TV Papa had bought for him and placed between the two front seats, with a stack of Disney CDs. Not having a planed route, Papa Jim asked Mike if he had ever been to New Orleans and he said no. So, instead of turning north on I-65 in Mobile Alabama, Papa Jim headed straight west to show little Mike, the Big Easy. Even though they never stopped or got out of the car, Papa Jim pointed out things to remember, like the Mississippi River, the French Quarter, and the Super Dome, only after the quick tour of the sights, did he cut over to I-55 and all points north. Papa Jim learned, much to his surprise that Mikey could sing pretty well, laugh out loud and ask a lot of questions.

Memphis, Tennessee came up on the horizon just as the sun went down, so they pulled into a large Holliday Inn with a sign promoting an indoor swimming pool. After a nice dinner in the restaurant, they headed for the heated pool along with some other small children that were there with their parents. They all played with a small rubber ball that Papa would throw up in the air so Mickey and the other kids could chase it down and retrieve it from the bottom of the pool.

Early the next day Papa got Mikey up, dressed, and down to breakfast where Mikey told papa, he never eats breakfast. Papa insisted he have some eggs and toast explaining how they had a long drive to St. Louis, but Mikey said that if he ate, it would make him sick. Papa would have none of that and insisted he at least eat something to which Mikey said "OK but I will be sick." About 75 miles north of Memphis, Papa discovered Mikey was a man of his word, as he projected his breakfast all over the back seat, himself, and the drivers head rest. Papa had no choice, he pulled off the road and got Mikey and his car seat out, cleaned them both up with a bottle of water and some paper towels. He got Mikey's suitcase out of the trunk and while standing on the side of the road behind the car, stripped off all his clothes, cleaned him up and put new clothes on him. Papa is still sure many of the cars that passed by are still talking about what they saw on that cold winter day along northbound highway I-55. Lucky for Papa there were no cell phones back then.

They finally arrived in St. Louis where they both had a wonderful time visiting with the cousins and their aunts and uncles. They took a paddle boat trip up the Mississippi River from the St. Louis landing near the Arch, went to the Science exhibit, and have the pictures to prove it. On the trip home, they once again stopped at that large motel with the indoor pool, but this time they skipped breakfast.

The honest observations of our children often provide us with smiles that last a lifetime. As you read this story keep in mind, this is the son of the young six year old boy that honestly, but accidentally told the manager of the St. Louis Cardinals he was ready to play.

DOUBLE TROUBLE

by James E. Fell

Mikey was over to visit Papa one day when Papa lived at Destin Sands a condominium right on Destin Harbor. Although Papa and his landlady, Jeanne would later get married, at that time they were just friends. Jeanne kept her pontoon boat at Destin Sands and let Papa use it. While Papa and Mikey were eating lunch that day, the phone rang and it was Jeanne. She told Papa her twin sister from Baton Rouge was in town and they would like to use the boat but she wanted to be sure Papa didn't have plans. He told her he wasn't planning to use the boat but needed a few minutes to clean it up.

When Papa hung up the phone, he showed Mikey a business card that was on the refrigerator door with Jeanne's picture on it and explained that she was the lady that owned the boat and would be over soon to pick it up and they needed to go out to the dock and clean it up. Papa forgot to tell Mikey that Jeanne had a twin sister. While Papa was checking out the motor and fuel tanks Mikey was on the front of the boat picking up life preservers and putting them under the seats. A few minutes later Mikey looked up, saw Jeanne and her twin sister Deanne walking down the dock towards the boat. Both confused and excited, he turned and shouted, Papa, Papa, she's here, and there's two of them."

Just like her mother, "sweet Angee," Lilly is now the middle child and just like her mom, hopelessly locked between two brothers.

A BLONDE IN HER FUTURE

by Angela Brumfield

The entire Brumfield family became diehard St. Louis Cardinal Baseball fans when Mark McGuire, their famous hitting star, was competing to break the age old record, held by Babe Ruth, for the most home runs in a single season; 60.

When that day finally came and McGuire hit number 61, Josh, her older brother, was explaining this great feat to his little sister. Lilly listened intently and when Josh told her that Mark McGuire had broken Babe Ruth's record, her innocent response was, …"Did he get in trouble?"

All I can tell you about this next story is that, it is true. It really did happen to Josh and Luke, the sons of "Sweet Angie" and Mikey, the son of her brother, Jimmy.

DO YOU BELIEVE IN ANGELS

by Angela Brumfield

When my son Josh was small, he had bad dreams quite often and he would wake up crying. Josh's grandmother, my mother had died before any of her grandchildren were born, but I had a picture of her and put it on Josh's dresser next to his bed. I told Josh "this was your grandmother who is now your guardian angel and she will watch over you and protect you at all times." From that day on, Josh had no more bad dreams.

One Christmas, several years later, Josh's aunt Carolyn and uncle Jimmy, came with their children to visit. The boy cousins, Mikey and Trey stayed with Josh in his bedroom. Neither Mikey, or any of the other members of his family, had ever heard the story of Josh's bad dreams or his guardian angel. The next day while the moms were in the bedroom cleaning up and the boys were helping make the beds, the mothers pointed to the picture of the lady on Josh's dresser and asked the boys if they knew who that was in the picture. Mikey immediately replied … that's the lady I saw standing in front of Josh's bed last night".

It has been said, there really are angels that look over us and protect us, but only the very pure of heart, ever see them.

The following is an Email message from Papa Jim to his wife Jeanne, and is all about six year old Landry, the daughter of the engineer that took our swimming pool cleaning equipment apart when he was just 10 years old.

THE COLOR PURPLE

by Jeanne Fell

Dear Jeanne,

Mike left work early yesterday. He told me he had to go to school to talk to Landry's teacher. The teachers at her school have a very clever way of letting the parents know how their child is doing at school. They use color code boxes at the top of the papers that they bring home. The teacher colors the box purple if the child has done very good that day, green if average, and red if they have not paid attention, talked during class or just goofed off.

Landry apparently had figured all this out and decided she would prevent a lot of grief at home, by just finding a purple pen and using her artistic talent along with a little color therapy to fix up her reports before she brought them home.

Landry is on serious "time out"

Remember "Big Wheels?" This is another story about his daughter Landry, the one that doctored up her report cards with the color purple.

DON'T EAT THE CRABS

by James E. Fell

Landry Fell

Landry's dad bought a crab trap, baited it with chicken parts, and dropped it in the water over the edge of their boat dock. Each day, Paxton and his little sister Landry, would go down to the docks, pull up the trap to see if they had caught a crab. One day they pulled up the trap and found they had captured a full grown blue crab. Their dad suggested they keep it in the trap and see if it would attract more crabs. Each day Paxton and Landry would check the trap, feed the one crab they had caught, played with it and even gave it a name.

After about a week Landry's dad said "I don't think we are going to get another one, so let's take this crab up to the house, cook it and have it for dinner". Paxton was excited because he wanted to see how it would taste and even more importantly, wanted to know what that crab was made of. But poor little Landry was sobbing out of control, while pleading with them, not to eat the crab. Still sobbing and crying, she threw herself on the dock in front of Paxton and her dad's pathway to the kitchen. They simply stepped over her and continued toward the house. As loud as her little voice could manage, she shouted after them, "this crab is special, it's like family." She continued to sob and laying there on the deck she made one final plea as they walked away, "we eat crabs from Winn-Dixie!... We don't eat, family."

Remember when we said "Every parent constantly sees things their children do that are little clues as to what they may do when they grow up." That was a story about big Mike, Paxton's father, but as they say, "the rest of the story" is that big Mike, actually did become an engineer.

Now that you know what happened to Mike, read about his son Paxton in the second generation stories called "Piano Player or Engineer.

PIANO PLAYER OR ENGINEER

by Jeanne Weeks Fell

Paxton Fell

One day Mike and Keeley dropped Paxton off to stay with us while they went shopping. All children that come to Papa's house will sooner or later migrate to the baby grand piano and Paxton was no different. Unlike the other children that use the piano as a noise toy and think the harder they hit the keys the louder the sound, Paxton had a very soft touch and he would actually seek out melodies such as Happy Birthday or Jingle Bells.

On this day, while Paxton worked at seeking out a song on the baby grand, Papa and Jeanne went into the next room to fix the computer. They could hear Paxton playing but the notes had become singular and repetitive. Curious, they stepped back into the living room and saw Paxton standing on the piano bench looking down into the strings and hammers while at the same time playing the same note over and over. It was obvious Paxton wanted to know just what makes this thing work and it made us wonder, … piano player or engineer?

Being a cancer survivor, Nancy always ends her letters, emails, and short stories with a quotation from Louisa May Alcott's book, "Little Women." Her story "Someday" will help explain why she selected the quotation she did.

SOMEDAY

by Nancy Fell Murphy

"You will make a wonderful mom someday". I wish I had a penny for every time I heard this said during my younger years. Although, if someone had told me, God had a different plan for me, I would not have accepted such a prognosis, not even for a moment.

I grew up in a suburb of St. Louis, Missouri where the average family had between four and five kids, my family was no exception. We not only had five biological siblings, we had more. We had today, what some would call "a functionally dysfunctional family." After six years of trying, my parents could not wait for me, they took on two brothers in foster care two years before I was born. They continued to be part of our family, even while my mom gave birth to four more children; three brothers and my sister, Angie. Even seven wasn't the final number. When one day, our babysitter's mom unexpectedly died and her father announced he was moving to New York, she asked if she could stay with us. So instead of her leaving, she also became a part of our family, and stayed all through her high school years. She was deservedly promoted from *babysitter* to *big sister*. Although this may seem strange to some, it was a wonderful family to grow up in with lifelong memories of very loving and fun filled times together. Through all this, I had the perfect role model for parenting from a mother who exemplified the perfect "Mother of the Year," every year.

My earliest recollection of caring for children came when my mom allowed me to "watch" my younger siblings, when the big kids were away, or when she had to run next door to a neighbors for a few minutes or to the store. This small job later became a stable income for me, when my mom began trusting me more and even paying me to baby sit while she ran to the shopping center just up the street, or to watch them while she got her hair done. I was just beginning to comprehend this responsibility thing, which probably went straight to my head, because the first day my younger brother, Jimmy, decided he no longer needed to take orders from me, was the last day of baby sitting my siblings. Suddenly, I was out of a lucrative job. At the ripe old age of nine, I was broke and unemployed. I was sure I still wanted to take care of kids, but I preferred them never to have the same last name as mine. What was I to do?

Luckily, we lived next door to a growing family whose family room was completely surrounded with windows and could easily be monitored from our deck or family room. Moms are so clever. One day, I was formally asked to come over and babysit the O'Neill children for the evening. I was only ten, but I was so proud and felt very adult-like to be a "real baby sitter."

Looking back on this now, I believe my mom and Mrs. O'Neill had planned the whole thing as a practice run under the "microscope of the all glass family rooms", so they could check on me but at the same time give me confidence and affirm my commitment to responsibility. I am sure they were only gone for about an hour, but to me it seemed like the entire day. I felt so good, being the caregiver for two adorable little kids. I was on top of the world. I think I kept that crisp one dollar bill they gave me for the better part of the following year. I loved to hold it and feel the pride ooze out, with the thought that it was earned doing just what I loved to do best. As the years went on, I continued to babysit for our neighbors, and as I got older my reputation preceded me. I was getting calls from all the moms in the neighborhood as well as a few of my mom's friends all around town. More often than not, after a sitting job, I would hear those magic words, *"You will be such a good mother someday."* Those words resonated loudly in my ears, and sparked my motherhood button. I even started thinking of the names for my own children. I wanted my children to have perfect names, to remind me of the perfect and cute children I sat for. Of course, when I sat for a child who was uncooperative or just plain mean, I would delete that name from my mental file of baby names. I couldn't wait until I was an adult, became a mom, and have a family of my own.

In the fall of 1977, my family participated in a church retreat designed for families, called "Family Weekend Encounter". It was a partnership with "Marriage Encounter." On this one particular weekend, we were in Kansas City, Missouri. As part of our team, a priest came along to provide spiritual support for the weekend. Our priest was Father Jim, and as I recall he was a quiet man, but very observant. He was always watching everyone, but at the same time appeared to be in deep thought or prayer. In one of our activities, they had each of us select the name of a family member, and make that person a very special gift, that represented the gifts that person brought to you and what gifts you bring to that person. When we finished the project, each person had to get up in front of everyone and present the homemade tribute they had made from scraps found in an arts and crafts box. You had to explain why you made that gift for them. I remember with some guilt, spending more time on the making of the gift, than the purpose for the gift. When it came time for our team's gift presentation, my family sat waiting for our individual turns. Father Jim had joined our family for this project, and he went first. I remember him standing there with a folded green craft paper card, and my 13 year old mind thinking, "Wow, he sure didn't put much effort in making that gift; I sure hope it is not mine!" In hindsight, little did I know that card was about to be one of the best gifts I would ever receive. He started by saying my name, and then describing the most amazing woman who would have the perfect family and the perfect life. He had glued a picture of a family with a beautiful mom, good looking dad and two of the most perfect looking kids on bikes riding together. Inside the card he wrote how he could see me when he looked at the picture of this family, and knew "I would make a perfect mom someday." At thirteen, my self esteem shot sky high. I knew he must be a prophet, because he worked for God. I knew I would treasure that moment for a lifetime. I then returned home to my daily routine and my dreams of becoming a mother one day.

As the years passed, I continued to be one of the neighborhood's preferred sitters, and even ventured out one summer with a close friend, Patti, to start our own Children's Day Camp right in our back yard. It was a huge success, except for the day a realtor lady asked us to keep the children "out of sight," while she showed the house next door. She explained that the woman looking at the house was not fond of children. I could not believe anyone, especially a woman, could not be fond of children, and even if she wasn't, this was not the neighborhood for her. The water seemed to have fertility drugs added to it that produced an average of four kids per household. As luck would have it, she bought the house, but it wasn't long after she moved in, my father was transferred to Florida and we were gone, but my love for kids and my dream for children of my own, stayed with me.

As a teenager living in ‘Florida, as fate would have it, I once again became the neighborhood babysitter. Just like in St. Louis, the same words rang from the mouths of the new parents, “what a wonderful mother you will make someday.” I began to look at my potential boyfriends as genetic donors and sometimes selecting them on the grounds of the beautiful babies we could make. When I entered college, my first big summer job was as a nanny for a large family. It was not only fun, it was the first time I really felt like I was actually being a “mom,” with two continuous weeks of doing what I loved best.

Then after I graduated and became a full time teacher, I would take summer jobs staying with families while their mom and dad took well deserved vacations. When they returned to see their children were fine and had done well without them, these moms would jokingly say, they hoped I would never meet Mr. Right for fear of loosing me to my own family.

As each year passed, I began to sense things were not going according to my plan, and I frequently would have long chats with God--about how things were supposed to happen. “I would make a wonderful mom!” Had He not heard these people? I began thinking about adopting a child on my own. Everyday I felt another egg get older; my biological clock ticking so loud, it bothered the neighbors.

At age 35, reality hit. I realized it may never happen. As sad as I was, realizing I may not have the family I had dreamed of or become the mom that I thought I would be, I prayed that God would find a way of easing the pain and He did. He introduced me to my husband, Gary. There was still a slight glimmer of hope, but after a series of serious health problems over the next few years, I knew the doors had actually closed for me to have children through medicine or adoption. This was not easy to accept, and once again I went through some very tough times. I began to ask myself, “in the big scheme of things, who ever said motherhood could only be defined as one who gives birth, or one who hears the word “Mommy,” lovingly called out in the middle of the night?”

I discovered there are other kinds of moms. I have had a most wonderful experience being *a special kind of mother*, more than I could ever have asked for. I will never be another Mother Teresa, but, as she once said, “I had many children, in my eyes” and now I understand how that can be. My sister, my brothers, my close friends, and my students have truly blessed me with true feelings of motherhood. I have twelve biological nieces and nephews and many close friends whose children lovingly refer to me as "Aunt Nancy." I have had a few students, two in particular, that have allowed me to become a very important part of their lives for the past sixteen years, and I plan to be there for them much longer. I also have two very special Jack Russell Terriers, Skip and T.J., who bring joy to me every day. They have taught me the reason for unconditional love in everyone's life.. So once again when I look back on my life, I ask myself … was this what being a wonderful mom was all about … not exactly? Did I loose anything because of God's real plan for me?...not really. I no longer look at it the same way. Did I gain anything from this experience with my own special kind of motherhood…Absolutely? I am very happy with my life, and the special kind of "mom" I have been able to be. Some days are still hard for me, but I know now my life has a purpose. I am finding hidden joy, being an aunt, a confident, a trusted friend, and deeply honored that some parents have even named me as their children's Custodial Guardian.

I know in my heart, I would have been a good mom if I had been given the birth opportunity. But, as a "Pseudo Mom", I know I have done a pretty good job. and as we all know, "Someday" never really comes, simply because, "someday" is always with us … everyday.

"I'm not afraid of storms, for I am learning to sail my ship."

From *Little Women* by Louisa May Alcott

Although Nancy Murphy is a cancer survivor, and has been a victim of rheumatoid arthritis since she was sixteen, she is also a teacher for hearing impaired children, a volunteer for everything and above all, a survivor. She started her writing career with e-mails called "Lymph Notes" while taking her first round of chemo. Her new Blog is called "Because of Daisies" and was inspired by her mother who died when she was very young. Her story begins with the introduction of her new Blog and explains how she came up with the title.

BECAUSE OF DAISIES

My story is probably no more unique, in many ways, than anyone else (everyone has a story), but I felt the need to tell my story about how God brought me through with the help and strength of my family of caregivers. He has blessed me with my life through my faith in Him. Therefore, starting with my mom, I am going to dedicate each story I write to a person who has been in my life for a reason, a season, or a lifetime.

Although she has been gone for sometime now, the inspiration for the name of my Blog came from my mom. She gave me the faith that has given me the perseverance and strength to hold on to my sail even when the wind is blowing me off my ship! She may not be here to read my words, but there is no doubt in my mind she still helps to inspire them just as she helps me wake up every single day and thank God for the strength to keep going. With her inspiration I finally came up with a name for my new Blog, **"Because of Daisies."**

Daisies were my mom's favorite flower---hence, the reason my spare bedroom is done in daisies, my office cubicle, the flowers in my wedding, and now my Blog. Most importantly, she is the reason I collect a daisy for every chemotherapy treatment and each bone marrow biopsy I am "graced with. So whenever I am having a tough day or making a hard decision, I look to my vase of flowers and think --- Because of Daisies---I can do it! I would never have thought a little daisy, which stands for innocence; purity and cheerfulness could be such a powerful symbol in my life.

The following story was taken from the January 24th entry in her blog, "Because of Daises" and is dedicated to her husband Gary.

THE BUTTERFLY EFFECT

by Nancy Fell Murphy

"*It is what it is*". How many times have you heard this saying and not even thought twice about the real meaning? When do you say it and mean it, is it actually saying there is nothing you can do about it…but, what if you could change "It"?

While I sat with my husband in the examination room, waiting for the doctor to come in and confirm what we already knew—"it's" cancer … (again). So many things ran through my mind, as I let the reality sink in, but settled on one single thought; what if I could only go back in time, and the nagging question, "what if...?" Ok, so if a person could go back in time—does one go back a few months, a few years, or a few decades?

"The Butterfly Effect" is a metaphor describing a small change at one point in time to a complex system, such as a person's life, that can have large effects on the future. It was featured in a movie, "The Chaos Theory," and, if you saw the movie with the same name, you know how convoluted the results can be. It is basically a theory explaining how everything in your life may have an effect on the past, the present, and ultimately; it can completely change the entire outcome of the future. So, if, I was to go back and change how I ate, where I lived, what medicines I took, or what environmental factors I was exposed to, would it take away the cancer? Possibly, but then, would I still live in Florida? Would I be teaching Deaf and Hard of Hearing children? Would I be married to Gary? See, it could indirectly affect every aspect of my entire life?

Recently, while talking with my very dear friend, Natalie, who also has successfully conquered two bouts with Cancer, I was relieved to hear that she could relate to these feelings. She recognized the fact that God did have a special plan for us through the trials we have been given. He is in control of our past, present and future. We both agreed there are surprising effects from the cancer-- both good and bad, but sharing our experiences with others, to grow and change was helpful. We each said, going through this is still a personal and unique experience, especially in the cases where there is the possibility it could be terminal-- you look at life differently. It is a gift, and a burden, in a weird way. In a strange sense, this is one of "the benefits" of being diagnosed; it is as if God gives us a special glimpse into our past, present and future, all at once. There are some things you don't ever think you will have to think about, until the time comes. But, if given that time, even for a brief moment, you automatically think about them and they can change your perspective on everything in a flash.

So I want you to think of the Butterfly Effect as something different in the face of any kind of life-altering adversity, like cancer. It is a chance to change the future, not the past. It follows one of my favorite truisms: **"Just when the Caterpillar thought its' life was over, it became a Butterfly!"** Just like the Caterpillar--the trials and tribulations that will come from cancer will make us all become a better person just for having experiencing "it".

There comes a time when we all need to just stop looking at our past, guessing about our future and try not to tell our mind what our heart wants to say. Sooner or later we must accept the fact that "It is what it is" and "that" is our gift from God.

This blog is offered to anyone going through any form of adversity and to all their caregivers--may they also find "a new beginning." But most of all, I want to dedicate this story to a very special caregiver, my loving husband, Gary, who has been in this cocoon with me for the past 8 years, and is very patiently waiting for the Butterfly to finally be released. Thank you so much Gary for all the love and support that will allow us to make this, another new beginning!

Fly Butterfly, fly.

"I 'am not afraid of storms, for I am learning to sail my ship"

From Louisa May Alcott's, Little Women

For weeks I pondered the question of how one buys Christmas gifts for adult children who have everything. Before you laugh yourself silly about the "having everything" part, listen to what your father has to say about giving. My solution was to write them the following letter.

TO ALL MY CHILDREN

by James E. Fell

MY CHILDREN,

Real gifts, are those things you give when you give something of yourself, something you made just for them. Don't worry, I'm not going to knit you a sweater.

I have written each of you some short stories about my recollections of your adventures growing up with your mom, your dad, and four sibling rivals. Those were happy times, sad times and loving times, but most of all they were family memories – the ones that will always remind you that, "you really do have everything". Merry Christmas

I have ended the "Nibletts with something I wrote for my children and grandchildren. Now I offer this simple lesson of life to all that wish to know what I have found to be, "the truth".

THIS I BELIEVE

by James E. Fell

No one lives over seventy years and learns nothing about life or fails to find something worth believing in. And if there is wisdom in age, who deserves to share in that knowledge more than our children? This is why I write, to tell you what I have found to be the truth and where it will lead you.

The most important and most valuable thing any person can own is a simple faith in a deity. Follow this faith and let it set the basic values for your life and it will give you the rules to live by. It is only when we trade these values for fear and doubt that we began to believe our problems are beyond resolution.

Many times in my life I have failed. I thought life was unfair and hopeless, until I found the answer. If you ever feel this way, go to a quite place and pray for people who have real problems, and real handicaps that make yours pale in comparison. God loves an honest doubter, but when you have doubts, stay in that quiet place and ask yourself; if you were to die tomorrow, what would you do with the remainder of this day? And before you leave that quite place; be sure to once again, dedicate your life to something more important than yourself.

As a famous journalist once said "You are the only person alive who has sole custody of your life – not just the life of your mind, but the life of your heart – not just your bank account … but your soul."

All my life's experiences and life's lessons have been reduced to just these few words and even these few words would be totally worthless without actions to back them up. LOVE, DAD

www.ingramcontent.com/pod-product-compliance
Ingram Content Group UK Ltd.
Pitfield, Milton Keynes, MK11 3LW, UK
UKHW041933190726
13854UKWH00004B/1561